TALES FROM THE
MONTREAL CANADIENS
LOCKER ROOM

A COLLECTION OF THE GREATEST
CANADIENS STORIES EVER TOLD

ROBERT S. LEFEBVRE

SPORTS
PUBLISHING

Sports Publishing books may be purchased in bulk at special discounts for sales promotion, corporate gifts, fund-raising, or educational purposes. Special editions can also be created to specifications. For details, contact the Special Sales Department, Sports Publishing, 307 West 36th Street, 11th Floor, New York, NY 10018 or sportspubbooks@skyhorsepublishing.com.

Sports Publishing® is a registered trademark of Skyhorse Publishing, Inc.®, a Delaware corporation.

Visit our website at www.sportspubbooks.com

10 9 8 7 6 5 4 3 2 1

Library of Congress Cataloging-in-Publication Data is available on file.

ISBN: 978-1-61321-239-4

Printed in the United States of America

To the two Gerrys, who told the tales and passed the torch; to Howard C, who put me in the game, but believes all those damned lies; to Sparkle, who made my dream come true; to Miss JB, whose wrong thinking I could love anything more in life than her; to Peanut Wings, for her companionship and giggles throughout this process; to Dave and Mike, for giving my work a window; to SB and LW for their support and encouragement; and to Dylan, for being the last man standing.

TABLE OF CONTENTS

TABLE OF CONTENTS

TABLE OF CONTENTS

PROLOGUE

There are a countless number of books written about the Montreal Canadiens, their glory and their greatness. In addition, there are about two dozen or more biographies and autobiographies, of and by players. I don't know if it is a proud thing to boast of when stating that I have read a sizeable portion of them—but I have.

Not all of these books, but many, are a recounting of stories Canadiens fans are well familiar with: the 24 Stanley Cups; the dynasties; the Rocket's accomplishments and so on. I did not want to write a book that, for the most part, readers may already have read.

Having researched Canadiens' history extensively in my time, I have come to look at certain things differently. While I have great appreciation for the legend and the lore of the hockey club, I have often found that much is missing to complete a fuller story. I have also learned that much of the myth surrounding the team's popular perception is misleading at best.

When the opportunity to write this book came to me from the publishers, I was already three years deep working on another Canadiens-related project. During that span, I dug right back in time, to the old newspapers on microfilm dating as far as 1903. I've scoured them in both French and English, learning of the origins of the game of hockey in Montreal. I also learned that not everything regarding the Canadiens is as it appears to be. There are many perceptions which are inaccurate.

This book delves into those inaccurate perceptions, the myths that confound as often as they impress. Removing rose-colored glasses, another picture emerges. The club best known for being hockey's French-Canadian team is seen in a different light.

I hope that you enjoy the read.

Robert S. Lefebvre

INTRODUCTION

DECEPTIVE ORIGINS AND THE VERY FIRST GAME

The Montreal Canadiens are the most distinct of all hockey teams in North America, and the 24 Stanley Cups they have won play only a part of that assessment.

From the moment it announced its formation on December 4, 1909, the hockey club designated itself as being strictly French, seeking to fulfill what was then a longstanding local demand for a team representative of the language of the city's majority population. The ideal was a noble initial gesture, and with that nod the Canadiens were henceforth identified as hockey's French team. Such is how they have always been defined by the greater hockey community, and it is how they are forever to be envisioned. There is absolutely no getting away from it.

Much of their unique branding stems from having won as many titles as they have. Winning 24 Stanley Cups tends to have that effect. The rich past combined with the fact that they are the oldest professional hockey club in existence furthers their distinctiveness. The Canadiens are renowned worldwide, though in certain parts equally despised. Winning has that effect as well.

Further distinguishing the team, as well as helping contribute to the antipathy toward it, is the fact that their home base is situated in the lone Canadian province that has constitutionally declared itself as a distinct society. As the only hockey club on the continent to have been purposely created to satisfy a linguistic demand, the unique heritage is thereby translated into a restrictive definition, and with it comes specific expectations from a fanbase they must consistently cater to. They are condemned to forever attempt to remain as French as possible. They are cursed to win and damned if they fail. No other professional hockey club exists with such constraints. It is a skin impossible to shed.

But their history, their distinct origins and the reasons behind their success are badly misunderstood. Over time, myth has clouded truth and legend has embellished fact.

When it is stated that the Canadiens were created for the francophone population of Montreal, what that truly says is that they were originated to satisfy a specific demand from a large market.

Up until 1909, despite the large French majority in the city, there had never once been a hockey club composed strictly of French elements. The best players in Montreal had always been English. The francophone newspapers had, for quite a long time, bemoaned this fact. Since the establishment of the Stanley Cup in 1893, English Montreal teams known as the Amateur Athletic Association, the Victorias, the Shamrocks and the Wanderers had won the Cup a combined thirteen times. The French, understandably, wanted their own.

Hockey teams of the day consisted of seven players on the ice, plus a spare or two. The Montreal sports writers were in disbelief that finding seven quality French starters to compete against the English clubs could not be accomplished. There were countless French players available, and yet no team of strength had ever been put together as an official entry into any league or association. It had not come to be for a pair of reasons: Few figured they stood a chance; and the two best francophone talents spent their winters playing professionally in the International Hockey League, based in the Southern Ontario region and northern Michigan state.

The local press was hot on the topic of the fact that there was no French team when fate intervened and their wish came true in the late winter of 1909. Three coincidences had conspired to create a unique and rare opportunity: Jack Laviolette and Didier Pitre, players on the two Sault Sainte Marie teams in the IHL, saw their clubs eliminated from championship contention earlier than usual; a prolonged cold spell in Montreal allowed for quality ice conditions later than had been the norm; and the defending Cup champion Wanderers just happened to be seeking challengers in order to remain in game form for a defense of their title.

Within a matter of days, the press spearheaded the idea of an all-French club going up against the mighty Wanderers. The proposal was tendered in the papers and calls were made to players. The ice was quickly booked and the game announced for March 9. The historic match was highly anticipated, when fate took two more turns. The Wanderers lost a crucial game and were eliminated from Cup contention. They would play the game regardless. Several hours before the match, a winter storm hit the city, keeping all but 300 patrons and one newspaper reporter indoors. Not only would the Wanderers be a disinterested group for the game, but it would be attended only by the most ardent of francophone supporters.

Due to the weather conditions, one Wanderers player failed to show. Another two members had called it quits after the season, returning home to Western Canada. They would face the French team with only half their starters—and a few spares. Their opponents, billed as the French-Canadians in ads leading up to the game, wore the blue uniforms of the Montreal National club in the city league. They were composed of Pitre and Laviolette, a goalie named Coutu, and three other locals of some repute named Jetté, Dostaler, and Robitaille. Their rover was Newsy Lalonde, from the Toronto Professionals club. Together, they had put in one practice session to get acquainted.

The Wanderers had but one thing in mind for the contest, and that was to not lose and suffer humiliation at the hands of what was essentially a pickup team. It wasn't like they were at all worried, even with a depleted roster. The game began at a fast pace, with little checking or spent effort from the former champions. They took an early 3-1 lead—and then sat back and let the French squad come at them for all they were worth. Laviolette, Pitre and Lalonde all measured up, competing stride for stride with the best of the Wanderers players. They rushed at the goal continuously, often firing wide in furious haste. The teams alternated goals, with the Wanderers scoring almost at will. The French-Canadiens would then storm back, working tirelessly to come from behind. The half ended at 6-5 for the Wanderers, who were admittedly impressed by the skill that Laviolette, Pitre and Lalonde had demonstrated.

In the second frame, the Wanderers came out roaring, scoring four of the next six goals to put the game out of reach. They then sat back once more, allowing the French to make it close. In the end, Pitre scored four times and Lalonde added five, but the Wanderers emerged victorious by a score of 10-9. Intriguingly, the game featured not a single penalty call—a rarity for the time.

The following day, La Patrie gave a fairly honest rundown of the game, submitting the Wanderers' diminished desire as context. Over the next week, however, the other French Montreal dallies, who had no reporter in attendance, jumped aboard and spoke of a game for the ages. The Wanderers, it was then told, had barely escaped with the win, after the "National" team had given them all they could handle. The context then changed. The world champions were but one goal better than the French, and the dallies all agreed that with a little practice "we could take them."

Lo and behold, the excited exaggerations of the press worked marvelously. Soon, all of the French hockey community in Montreal was raving about a result few of them had seen in person. Furthermore, the euphoria maintained itself over the summer, and talk increased about the potential of having a French team in a newly created professional league.

But the raves and euphoria about the French powers were baseless, and the team's ascendance in the hockey world was hardly a testament to francophone hockey coming of age in Montreal. Laviolette was born in Belleville, Ontario, and had moved to Valleyfield, Quebec, as a young boy. There, he met Pitre, who was four years his junior. The pair became great friends, but then Pitre moved to Sault Ste. Marie in his early teens, where he would live year-round with his family, working and playing hockey. Lalonde, who scored five goals, was francophone in heritage only. He came from Cornwall, Ontario, and spoke not a word of French.

Despite their loose ties to the Montreal market, these three players together formed the basis for the creation of what would become the Montreal Canadiens nine months later.

On Saturday, December 2, 1909, in meetings at Montreal's Windsor Hotel designed to lay out the landscape for the professional hockey scene around the city, two spurned applicants for the Canadian Hockey Association became acquainted in the building's fabled hallways. They were Ambrose O'Brien, owner of the Renfrew hockey club, and Jimmy Gardner, the team captain and director for the Wanderers. Cast aside by the CHA core in their pursuit of both larger market teams with arenas of the biggest seating capacity, the men were in the process of plotting their own rival league when they realized they lacked one club to complete their plan. The CHA had admitted a French club to be known as Le National. Its creation was inspired by the March game in which Gardner had played, which had been greatly hyped ever since. After a meeting of the minds, O'Brien offered to bankroll a similar team for one season, to get their new league rolling.

They would call their rival league the National Hockey Association, and the team envisioned for French Montreal would be called Le Canadien.

1

1910-1935: MISCONCEPTIONS OF THE CANADIENS "FRENCH PLAYER TERRITORIAL RIGHTS RULE"—PART 1

Many Myths, Many Sides

Perhaps the biggest and most long-standing misconception concerning the Montreal Canadiens has to do with why they were such a dominant team during the Original Six period and the years immediately following it. The usual answers point to the team having been granted the exclusive right of ownership of all the best French players out of Quebec for years on end. Such a fallacy has been perpetrated for so long that it has practically become hockey folklore. The so-called privilege even has its own name, having long ago been cemented into the vocabulary of hockey culture with terminology along the lines of the Canadiens "French Player Territorial Rights Rule."

The trouble with this blanket assumption is that during the era of Original Six hockey (1942-1967), Canadiens were never granted such an exclusive, specific and unique clause. They were simply allowed by rule, as were the five other NHL teams, to sign players under the age of twenty playing in nonprofessional junior and senior leagues within a fifty mile radius of their home base. The Toronto Maple Leafs owned the exact same backyard privileges

1

in their region of Ontario, and this was also true as it applied to Boston, Chicago and New York in the United States and Detroit on both sides of the border. Of course, the other NHL franchises would have had virtually no French players within their respective radius limits, so it is only logical that the majority of francophone talent would be found within Montreal's region.

Were the best French hockey players around Montreal better than the best English-speaking talents from outside the province of Quebec? With the use of French players, the Canadiens won one more Stanley Cup than Toronto in the seasons between 1943 and 1967. The Maple Leafs' nine titles, as well as Detroit's five, were largely won with minimal contribution from Quebec-born players. Would either team have won more titles had they secured more French talent? Perhaps the Canadiens, whose rosters were every bit as English as French, would have won less often had they been forced to employ strictly French players. This is a valid theory, as up until the Original Six era, French players of substantial and equal skill were few and far between. The Canadiens had used them in bunches, and it never made them better.

About the only logical conclusion that can be reached is that the Canadiens won because they were able to use both French and English players. And there was never a ruling stating that any other NHL club couldn't employ the exact same tactic. Montreal's fifty-mile radius hardly encompassed all of Quebec's vast six hundred square miles. Good hockey players were found aplenty outside that fifty-mile parameter and were available to all teams. Few went looking, because historically there had been so few French players of quality to be found. Furthermore, there was always the apprehension by the English clubs to cultivate French players due to the language barrier. That type of thinking still exists in today's NHL. If such an aspect is still prominent today, it most certainly would have played into the thinking at the time.

Implausible as it may seem, for these reasons and others, their five Original Six partners would have wholeheartedly agreed, in 1942, to allow the Canadiens to have access to all the French players it desired. The appealing and mythical "Flying Frenchmen" brand existed well before the club became perennial beast slayers and they had always proven to be a popular draw at the turnstiles, in Toronto and the United States. Most importantly for the League, its existing alliance could only be as strong as its weakest link in the chain. That term best described the Canadiens at the end of the 1942 hockey season. Upon considering the proposal of territorial rights for its teams at that point, the NHL clubs as a whole had much more than the fortification of the Canadiens in mind. They wished to place their league on solid ground. It should never be forgotten that the six NHL clubs who survived the Great Depression were not completely out of the woods. The League was then staring down the prospect of a second world war. Given this, it was an instinctive survival reaction by the League to return to its roots.

The very notion of territorial player rights in sports is as old as sporting itself. Possibly every sporting league ever created began with homegrown players and residence rules. Just as team nicknames are often based on a region's particular characteristics, much of the allure for fans of any game is to cheer athletes who are representative of their region. Be it a matter of birthplace, ancestry, heritage or culture, sporting fans like to identify with their idols. The more hometown heroes, the better. It is why Dallas calls their NFL franchise the Cowboys and why Boston is represented in the NBA by the Celtics. Baseball has branded the Brewers, Marlins, and Astros to reflect their respective city's identities.

In Montreal, the combined aspects of birthplace, ancestry, heritage and culture took on very different meanings, with language becoming the most distinct identifier. It was the prime motivation behind its creation. The French press felt there was a need for a French hockey club, and necessity has forever been the mother of invention.

Given a deeper understanding, it can be seen that the Canadiens "French Player Territorial Rights Rule" is a pure myth that ought to have been debunked ages ago. That the Canadiens were unfairly advantaged is an opinion loaded with a pungent air of linguistic racial prejudice that has seemingly been passed down from generations of Canadiens-haters. Many journalists and authors have spoken of this rule as though it is an accepted fact, without ever investigating further into its background and improbability.

This is very easily done. One simple question is all it takes to poke holes into the notion as to why the Canadiens would be so exclusively and distinctly privileged: Why would five other NHL franchises, with overwhelming veto power on every single ruling, allow for a legislated ruling that continuously advantaged the Canadiens in beating them?

To properly explain and answer this question from every possible angle, it is first necessary to return to the exact moments of the Canadiens' creation in December of 1909.

In With the French—Out With the French

At the meeting that formed the NHL's predecessor, the National Hockey Association, the newly formed Canadiens club inquired and was granted the privilege of filling out their lineup with the best French-Canadian players available. As there were so few French players of elite skill level at the time, the request was granted by NHA partners with barely a second thought. The Canadiens finished with a 2-10 record over twelve games that first season. The NHA in 1909 (and later, the NHL) never bothered to specifically define in its constitution exactly what qualified a player as being French-Canadian. Whether it is either the ability to speak the language, a player's place of birth or his family heritage is not outlined in published NHA constitutions for the following season.

No longer owned by Renfrew's Ambrose O'Brien in their second season, the franchise now known as the Club Athletique Canadien had to pay their former owner for the rights to star Newsy Lalonde, who was considered as the first of the long lineage of Flying Frenchmen. During 1909-10, O'Brien owned four of the leagues' seven clubs, and he had cunningly released Lalonde from his Canadiens contract in order to sign him to Renfrew. After close to two months of haggling and a high ransom fee, the Canadiens did get Lalonde back, but the NHA never clarified whether he was ruled as belonging to Renfrew due to a newly enacted reserve player clause in April 1910, or because he was French only in heritage and did not speak the language.

By their third season, the Canadiens were openly signing English players to improve their standing, which upset other clubs who found the arrangement unfair. An agreement was thereby reached for the 1912-13 season allowing the Canadiens to dress two English players per game, while other NHA clubs could dress two French players.

4

This then provided the other clubs with the option of signing French players ahead of the Canadiens should they choose to. Once more, this newest wrinkle was never specifically written into the constitution and remained little more than a gentleman's agreement. It appeased, for all intents, the unfairness of a rule that in some opinions allowed the Canadiens to double-dip into two talent pools.

With hindsight, the ruling was beyond inconsequential for the other NHA teams. For the most part, players of French language or heritage were practical nonentities on the rosters of the Wanderers and Senators. The Wanderers were Montreal's English team of note, and the rivals of the French were not about to dress francophone players to the great displeasure of their fans. Ottawa, on the other hand, could easily have promoted French talent to their squad. A good size of their population was bilingual and their countless inner city league teams contained several quality francophone players. Still, for reasons unexplained, they shunned the French. The city of Toronto, new to the NHA at this time, swelled with quality English players, enough to fill two pro teams and several feeder leagues. They had no need for the French.

The Stanley Cup champions of 1912 and 1913 were the Quebec Bulldogs. It could be assumed that they had the greatest interest in blocking the Canadiens exclusive right to French players, but they were largely indifferent to the issue. The roots of the Quebec club threaded back to 1880, and they existed in a government city that still had a large contingent of English residents by the 1910s. During their two-year championship run, their roster, filled with English surnames, reflected that fact. It included Harry Mummery and Joe Hall of Brandon, Manitoba; Ontario-born players such as Goldie Prodgers (London), Eddie Oatman (Springford), Tommy Smith (Ottawa) and Jack Marks (Brantford). Three local players, Joe Malone, Jack McDonald and Paddy Moran, were born in Quebec City.

What the Quebec club had in common with the Toronto franchises, the Wanderers and Ottawa, was that they were English-owned and operated. Not only were they getting by dressing few French players, they were winning Stanley Cups. As far as they were concerned, the Canadiens could have all the Frenchmen they could find. There weren't very many who were seen as being good enough, and teams were winning without them. The whole of the

French question was a nonstarter for all professional NHA teams. It is of little wonder then, why the NHA and the NHL never bothered to have regulations concerning French players constitutionally defined or properly explained in local newspapers.

Thus, it can be stated without much debate, that the Canadiens' first brief period of exclusive French player rights resulted in little positive effect. Nonetheless, the Canadiens carried on, needing the French element less and less as they became more successful. Upon winning their first Stanley Cup in 1916, their roster of thirteen players was split almost down the middle between players of French and English heritage. A half-dozen French-speaking players on the championship team included: Georges Vézina of Chicoutimi, Quebec; Georges "Skinner" Poulin, born in Smiths Falls, Ontario; Jack Laviolette, born in Belleville, Ontario; Didier Pitre of Valleyfield, Quebec; Louis Berlinguette of Papineau, Quebec; and sub Jack Fournier, birthplace unknown. Six English Ontario-born players consisted of: Skene Ronan of Ottawa; Amos Arbour of Waubaushene; George "Goldie" Prodgers of London; Bert Corbeau of Penetanguishene; and brothers Harold and Howard McNamara of Randolph. Edouard "Newsy" Lalonde, of francophone heritage but born in Cornwall, led the group. The linguistic complexion of the Canadiens would change little for close to thirty seasons.

As the NHA became the National Hockey League prior to the start of the 1917-18 professional hockey campaign, all that would change in terms of constitution for the moment would be the banner name topping all League documents. The newly named four-team league adopted the NHA constitution and rulebook in whole, and there were no updates or specially defined provisions for the Canadiens regarding their right to French players. With the NHL losing the Montreal Wanderers four games into the season due to a fire at their shared Westmount arena home, the Canadiens were left as the lone professional hockey club in the city. Though the heated rivalry between the Canadiens and Wanderers and their respective fans had never wavered, in recent seasons the Canadian Arena Company (CAC)-owned team's stock had risen, while the English team's standing skidded toward a free fall.

After the fire, the Canadiens returned to play at the Jubilee Arena, their former home, but the Wanderers, already in financial straits, abandoned play and their players were dispersed among the remaining three teams. Although the Canadiens had veered away from the original mandate of an all-French club, players of francophone heritage such as Lalonde, Vézina, Laviolette and Pitre remained in their ranks, and that seemed to be all that the majority of the population required to continue supporting the team. Sweeping changes were on the horizon for hockey in general, but it would hardly affect how the Canadiens would go about their business.

The American-Born Dandurand and the Flying Frenchmen Myth

From 1910 on, the Canadiens had been owned by the Canadien Athletic Club. Prior to the 1917-18 season, the club incorporated itself and the change in name to the Canadien Hockey Club was reflected in the alteration of its logo on team sweaters. Their director, George Kennedy, was a bilingual Irishman who had gained his reputation as a promoter in the local wrestling medium. Despite being head of the CAC, Kennedy's investment into the sporting realm and the hockey club itself were largely backed by dozens of local businessmen, including a pair of very prominent French newspaper magnates. These investors placed profit well ahead of other concerns, and the language spoken by its hockey players was never the highest priority as long as the team kept winning. From the time of its first Stanley Cup in 1916 to the team's fourth crowning in 1931, the Canadiens made it to the League final eight times, winning six NHL championships and missing the playoffs on only four occasions. During this span, the issue of the Canadiens signing few French players was rarely of concern. Their English stars were top caliber, and as there were no superior French players to be found, fans were at least pleased to see a dash of locals scattered among the talent on a highly entertaining, quality hockey club.

George Kennedy passed away in 1921, at which time his full ownership of the franchise was sold to Léo Dandurand and two business partners. Dandurand, an American-born francophone, was as well versed in sports promotion as Kennedy had been. Somewhat more worldly, Dandurand was perfectly prepared for the challenges that lie ahead for the Canadiens and the League as a whole. The NHL was about to move into the United States, and Dandurand's promotional abilities deftly assisted this forward step. He helped brand the Canadiens as "Les Habitants" and the "Flying Frenchmen," and though both terms were slight misnomers, Dandurand has been credited as the first person to bring a certain myth and French mystique to the greater perception of the Canadiens.

Through his American newspaper connections, Dandurand began to expertly promote the Canadiens' appeal as a group of distinct individuals playing a barnstorming brand of hockey. He was greatly aided in these endeavors by the exploits of two of the game's fastest rising stars in Aurèle Joliat and Howie Morenz. He completely fabricated tales about his players, such as the one concerning the prowess of goalie Vézina fathering 22 children, including three sets of triplets in just nine short years. The press and fans alike ate it up and just had to see these Canadiens to believe the stories.

As the NHL looked to set up shop in American cities, Dandurand brought the Canadiens to such places as Boston, New York and Chicago in order to promote both the team and the game itself. Exhibition matches were played with a host of varying adversaries, and Dandurand relished a share of the box office receipts. Encountering the U.S. press, the owner allowed only a few select French players to speak to journalists in broken English, so as to not dispel any myths. The jig would have been exposed had anyone spoken to Joliat or Morenz and discovered their perfect English tones. Boston was the first U.S. city to gain an NHL club in 1924 and when the Canadiens first visited, their sweaters were emblazoned with a globe logo, replacing the familiar CH crest. The signification for "World Champions" was hardly subtle, but the gesture, combined with the mythologizing of the team in the press beforehand, worked advantageously. Soon, the Canadiens had offers to make stopovers in other cities, where they would leave a lasting impression on those interested in the sport.

But the Canadiens championship club of 1923-24 was hardly worthy of being declared "Flying Frenchmen." Of the 13 players on the Canadiens that season, only three on the roster were truly francophone. Vézina of Chicoutimi remained from the 1916 champions. The goaltending great managed to speak broken English at best. Joe Malone, now in his second stint with the Canadiens, was (despite his English surname), a francophone born in Quebec City.

Sylvio Mantha, a future captain and coach born in Montreal, was bilingual but spoke French as a first language. The remaining ten players defied pure francophone qualification. Brothers Billy and Bobby Boucher were from Ottawa and were English-speaking despite their French surnames. Joliat, a player of Swiss descent acquired in the trade for Newsy Lalonde, was also from Ottawa. Sounding equally exotic in name was Howie Morenz, of Stratford, Ontario. Of German ancestry, Morenz would come to typify the earliest personifications of the Flying Frenchmen brand, while never coming near to commanding the language as Joliat had in a butchered French tongue. Nevertheless, Morenz's popularity was so grand that his opinions on hockey were translated into a weekly French print column, leading many to believe otherwise. Brothers Sprague and Odie Cleghorn were Montreal-born Anglophones. Billy Cameron was born in Timmins, Ontario. Bilingual Anglophone Billy Bell was from Lachine, Quebec, while Billy Coutu and spare Charles Fortier came from Sault Sainte Marie and Rockland, Ontario, respectively.

Though multitudes of decent to good French junior and senior players would demonstrate their playing ability in various city leagues around Montreal, inside Quebec, and outside of the province at this time, Dandurand's Canadiens found it difficult to unearth much valuable francophone talent of suitable skill level to play alongside the established NHL standard. Over the next five seasons, Montreal would dress eighteen players of francophone heritage from all parts. Only four would have any lasting impact.

The French players making the grade were Albert "Battleship" Leduc, Alfred "Pit" Lépine, Wildor Larochelle and Armand Mondou. Though none of these contributors personified the Flying Frenchman brand per se, they would each leave their mark on team history. Defenseman Leduc joined the club in 1925-26 at age twenty-two. Born in Valleyfield, Quebec, he would play nine seasons for Montreal, winning a pair of Stanley Cups. Joining him as rookies that same year were Lépine and Larochelle. The former was born in Bellevue, Quebec, and would perform mostly as the Canadiens second center for the next thirteen seasons. Winger Larochelle, from Sorel, Quebec, joined the team at age 18, and would stick with the club, mostly in defensive roles, for eleven seasons. In 1928-29, left winger Armand Mondou was judged as being ready for the big club.

A speedball skating blur, Mondou first toiled with the Providence Reds, an early Canadiens farm club. He then graduated to the Canadiens as a second-line offensive threat but had some trouble sticking with the Habs. Shuffled between the New Haven Eagles and the big leagues, Mondou would eventually leave his mark on NHL history as the first player to ever take a penalty shot.

The remaining fourteen players of French origin that the Canadiens considered in these five seasons were but passengers in the grander scheme of things. Rene Lafleur and Robert Joliat, Aurèle's brother from Ottawa, each played one game for the Canadiens in 1924-25. Hec Lepine, Alfred's brother, played 33 games in 1925-26. Twenty-year-old winger Roger Cormier dressed for one game only. Rollie Paulhus a defenseman from Sorel, registered no points in 33 games with Montreal and was returned to the Reds. Joe Matte, a player acquired from Boston, lasted a mere six games.

When goalie Vézina took ill during the first game of 1925-26 with a bout of tuberculosis that eventually claimed his life, Dandurand and the Canadiens thought they had properly prepared for his eventual succession. Looking ahead to the day when Vézina would retire, they signed 1924 U.S. Olympic team stopper Alphonse "Frenchy" Lacroix. Of francophone heritage, but born in Newton, Massachusetts, Lacroix was a bust on a team demoralized by Vézina's illness. Herb Rheaume, a 25-year-old goalie from Mason, Quebec, was brought in for the final 26 games, faring no better for the rudderless Habitants.

The 1926-27 team would see three more players of French origin join the club, two of them born in Ontario. Ottawa-born Art Gagné would score 41 goals in three seasons before moving on from Montreal to a career as a hockey journeyman. Art Gauthier, of Espanola, Ontario, would fill in at center for 13 games, and Léo Lafrance saw brief action in four contests. Neither player would return the following year. For 1927-28, the Canadiens would add two locals. Léo Gaudreault, a left winger from Chicoutimi would appear in 36 games. Charles Langlois did him one better, playing in 37 contests. Both were returned to Providence at season's end. Aside from Mondou, the lone new arrival in 1928-29 was Fall River, Massachusetts, native Art Lesieur. His contribution lasted slightly longer than other players of French heritage. Lesieur would shuttle back and forth from Providence, appearing in 98 games with Montreal in four separate seasons over eight years.

Part of the reason for the dearth of francophone talent on the club had to do with Dandurand's many sporting business interests. Not only did he own and coach the Canadiens, but his pursuits also extended into the realms of baseball, football and his ever-growing horse racing empire. The racetracks were Dandurand's most consuming passion. During his time behind the Canadiens' bench from 1921 to 1926, his efforts were largely dedicated toward improving the hockey club. It was during this period that he found such talents as Lépine, Larochelle and Leduc. Having set the Canadiens on solid ground, he then concentrated on his horse racing interests. He and his partners would eventually own over a dozen tracks, many of them in New York, Illinois, Delaware, Ohio and Louisiana. His constant treks into the United States account for his discovery of hockey talent in odd places and the establishment of the Canadiens' first affiliated farm club in Providence, Rhode Island. While the location proved convenient for the owner, it was far from an ideal area for displaced unilingual Quebec-born players to ply their trade.

While Providence was the primary destination for Canadiens hopefuls, Dandurand also had players scattered in various other places. From the mid-1920s until early in the coming decade, players signing contracts with Montreal were allocated to the CAHL's Québec Beavers, Newark Bulldogs, Windsor Hornets, the Niagara Falls Cataracts and the New Haven Eagles. There seemed no semblance of reasoning as to why players were sent to any particular place, but then again the art of grooming prospects during that period was much less scientific than it is today.

Connections, Good Fortune and Blarney

In any avenue of life, it pays to be in the right place at the right time. It is advantageous to be well-liked and to be associated with the right people. Networking results in the gathering of more information and the making of smarter choices. As the old adage goes, "It is all about who you know."

The method of scouting players and managing a hockey club was a radically different process in the 1920s. Scouts at the time were often the players, coaches and managers themselves, and the method generally involved little more than the passing along of tips on prospective talents. If a certain player sounded promising, a trip was then made to see the player in action and potentially sign him to a contract.

Léo Dandurand was an avid networker with a keen eye for spotting hockey talent. At this task, he was more than matched by Ottawa-born Tommy Gorman and Toronto's Conn Smythe and Frank Selke. Gorman was by then coming into his own as an elite hockey connoisseur. In the nation's capital, he had witnessed the process by which groups of competitive inner city league teams developed talent to feed the Senators' needs as well as the ability to identify quality talent at an early age. Many players who signed contracts with Ottawa had either played alongside or against each other at one time or another. Players they hadn't signed were constantly on Ottawa's radar simply based on how they measured up against the local talent. The competition was fierce, and it brought out the best in the hometown hopefuls wishing to move up to the big team. Smythe and Selke in Toronto took the same cues, as the exact process played out in their backyard with even larger quantities of players and teams involved. Ottawa's hockey club was by then a local institution for the city's sporting youth. Young children were growing up dreaming of becoming Senators one day.

In Montreal, however, Dandurand and the local hockey cognoscenti were much more latent in tapping into how to properly evaluate and groom talent. Little was being done to foster any form of player growth among the countless teams in Montreal's mess of inner city leagues. Rather than propose a similar setup to those in Ottawa and Toronto, it was all left alone to meander in the wilderness by provincial hockey associations. There remained large competitive gaps in the quality of teams of the same division. Structure was nonexistent, as clubs were often independently owned. Players of decent skill would beat up on weakened teams, padding what appeared to be impressive scoring totals. Annually, the best of this overestimated lot would receive invitations to try out for the Canadiens in order to earn a contract, lasting only a day or so while looking terribly out of step against the pros. It was a completely dysfunctional method of judging talent, and it continued for years on end without correction.

As recourse, the well-travelled Dandurand and Cattarinich were instead reliant upon their informed network of friends across many cities in almost every sport to keep them in good stead. Allies would pass on recommendations of players worthy of looking into and the Canadiens owners would often sign them on-site, based on a lone game evaluation. When it had come to financial matters and business opportunities, Dandurand had mostly relied on the purest of instincts gained from years of experience to serve him well. The same instincts and traits, however, were hardly transferrable as a method of tapping into hockey talent. His attentive ear, charismatic persuasion and deep pockets had come in handy on a few occasions, working in substitute of due diligence. As they benefitted him, Dandurand kept up a charade, essentially counting on luck to see him through. While the bluff allowed for lightning to strike twice and bring him three Stanley Cups, he would not notice the flaws inherent in proceeding in this manner for years, if, in fact, he owned up at all.

Late in 1921-22, Dandurand was at his wit's end with aging star Newsy Lalonde, then coach and captain of the Canadiens. The owner felt Lalonde was not giving his all, and though the pair was the best of friends off the ice, they began a running feud partway through the season. Léo had been the best man at Newsy's wedding years earlier, long before he had acquired the club from Kennedy. They often golfed together in the same foursome on weekends, a practice they would continue for forty years until Dandurand's passing in 1964. As sparks between the pair flew, Dandurand tore a strip off him in the press and the proud Lalonde promptly quit the team. He had been insulted by his owner's words. A parting of ways seemed inevitable, but Lalonde returned to the club, in a lesser role that better suited his battered 35-year-old body. All seemed to be settled when late in the following summer, Dandurand abruptly traded the soul of the Canadiens to the Western Canada Hockey League's Saskatoon Crescents. In doing so, he helped negotiate a sweetheart of a deal for Lalonde as Saskatoon's player-manager. Newsy was to get his biggest hockey paychecks out west, while Léo was raked over the coals for dealing the player that most represented Canadiens history up until that time. Why he did this had to do with something he had overheard that summer.

Aurèle Joliat was a rising star in the Ottawa hockey system, playing with the New Edinburg club in the city loop in the early 1920s. He became Senators' property along the way, and had been offered a contract by Gorman that was more than a little on the cheap side. Rather than signing, the rather feisty Joliat balked at what he felt was an insulting offer, vowing he'd rather sit out than play. Gorman promptly suspended and fined the cocky youngster from the Ottawa club and had him barred from playing in the NHL one year later on some very dubious charges. Joliat had laid low, playing only in exhibition games in Iroquois Falls, Ontario, and other locales. He had been accused of taking a large sum of gambling money in order to help throw a championship game. Pocketing the cash before hitting the ice, he then seemed to have a change of heart, filling the opposing net with pucks, and then bolted town by train—his skates still laced as he boarded. The story swirled through the hockey corridors as Joliat was nowhere to be found. The entire performance exposed his budding talent to all those in attendance, including one loyal Dandurand minion who reported back.

Cecil Hart was perhaps the finest evaluator of hockey talent in Montreal around this time. He had been associated with hockey in the city since 1910, operating a succession of inner city leagues. His family had been a staple of Montreal's financial business community for years, and though his hockey interests were purely a hobby for most of his early life, he was even better branched out than Dandurand when it came to keeping tabs on promising players. Through his wealthy family's investments, Hart was becoming involved in the Canadian Arena Company's plan to build the Montreal Forum. The Canadian Arena Company was to fill the building with an English team tenant that became the Maroons, and Hart was tagged to become its coach.

Well before the Maroons hit the ice, Hart was already pursuing players. He had learned of Joliat years earlier, and had wondered where he had vanished to. Knowing that he had been Ottawa property at one time, he inquired to Gorman about this, upon a chance meeting in Montreal. Dandurand apparently overheard the discussion between the two concerning the exiled Joliat's talent and current status as a pro. Learning that Aurèle had just then signed to play in Saskatoon, Dandurand got busy. Based on his scout's advice and Hart's conversation with Gorman, he rolled the dice and traded Lalonde out west for what an outraged Montreal press initially deemed an extremely unproved talent.

What Canadiens fans could not have known was that Joliat was practically a carbon copy of Newsy in gamesmanship and demeanor. Though Dandurand himself had never seen Joliat play, the fact that he was such an unknown quantity likely enabled him to have the NHL lift his ban and allow him to join the Canadiens at training camp. Wearing Newsy's number-four sweater, a leather cap and an ever-present devilish grin, Joliat helped the Canadiens reach the 1922-23 league final.

Hart helped out Dandurand even more, later that same season. This time it was on purpose. Hart had a falling out with the Maroons directorship and was no longer in their potential plans as manager. During December, there was a senior league tournament taking place in Montreal featuring a team from Stratford, Ontario. Alerted by a referee friend who was working one of the games, Hart was called out to the rink to witness the exploits of one Howard Morenz, who was busy tearing up a local side with a nine-goal performance. Hart then alerted Dandurand, who followed a week later to Stratford to see Morenz with his own eyes. He was immediately impressed and offered a contract on the spot, which the youngster thought best to think over. While there, Dandurand learned of the young man's debts, which were in the thousands. He wished to remain in town as his amateur salary and CNR apprenticeship were thought to be his best prospect for ultimately becoming debt-free. Come summer, when it was learned that the Maple Leafs were moving in on Morenz's rights, Dandurand quickly dispatched Hart to Stratford, offering a two-year salary that would cover every cent the player owed.

This shrewd maneuver by Dandurand, along with the risk taken on Joliat, helped provide the Canadiens with a stellar core for the coming decade. On both occasions, luck seemingly fell onto their laps, and Dandurand often regaled his company with tales of how he had acquired the pair he would later guise as the Flying Frenchmen. Though each deft move had as much to do with serendipity as it did with pure hockey smarts, the owner's success caused him to rest somewhat on his laurels.

Dandurand and the Canadiens' most pressing need coming out of the 1925-26 season was to find a suitable replacement for goalie Vézina. A sturdy solution was found in 32-year-old George Hainsworth, but as Dandurand often related the tale, it was Vézina himself who picked his eventual successor years before his passing. The pair had faced one another in an exhibition game four years prior, and Vézina liked what he had seen. The story behind his acquisition was a highly contested matter at the time. The Western Hockey League was folding, and complete team rosters were being sold in whole to expansion NHL teams in Chicago, Detroit and New York. Individual players not on those clubs were sold separately. A pair of NHL managers thought they had put in legitimate claims on Hainsworth's rights only to find out that Dandurand had signed him just days earlier.

The story of Vézina tipping him off became part of the Dandurand legend, but it is doubtful, to say the least, that any hockey club manager worth his salt would rely on a four-year-old secondhand assessment, even if it had come from Vézina himself. In fact, Dandurand might have received a much more profound evaluation from good friend Newsy Lalonde, who had played with and coached Hainsworth for three seasons.

Léo Dandurand is historically heralded as the Canadiens' first truly francophone club owner and manager, a fact ever so slightly misleading, as he was indeed American-born. During hockey's first major period of growth, his imprint is all over the branding of the Canadiens as the Flying Frenchmen and Les Habitants. In his fifteen-year reign as Canadiens owner, he not only fortified their standing, but he also turned the team into hockey's best and most popular club. He was an extremely valuable partner to the NHL as it expanded into U.S. territory. Dandurand, among his many accomplishments, not only left his mark on Canadiens history in Montreal, but he was also involved with the Montreal Nationals Lacrosse team and the Montreal Royals baseball team. Additionally, Dandurand founded the Montreal Alouettes football club and established the Blue Bonnets racetrack.

In 1952, a biography of his career, titled *Léo Dandurand—Sportsman* was published in French only. Written by Rosaire Barrette, the chronology of Dandurand's sporting life lists the names of hundreds of allies, which he made from the moment he set foot on Montreal soil. The book details how he landed in the city in the early 1900s with only a few dollars in his pocket, soon printing his own program lineups for games to sell at all sports events in order to make a few extra bucks. His quick rise to prominence in the Montreal sporting community is meticulously noted to the extent that it suggests that the book is practically a ghostwritten autobiography.

Sadly for fans of Canadiens history, the amount of hockey content discussed is rather minimal compared to the detailed narration of his other pursuits. The Canadiens hockey talk focuses mainly on such personalities as George Kennedy, Jos Cattarinich, Cecil Hart, Georges Vézina, Howie Morenz and George Hainsworth, all of whom were deceased by the time of publication. The living—Joe Malone, Newsy Lalonde, Sprague Cleghorn and others—are given little recognition in the Canadiens scheme. Lalonde, a lifelong friend, is more prominent in photos than actual text. Morenz is portrayed in a light that his family has often resented. Hart receives little credit in terms of his important contribution. Given the amount of attention paid to personal trivialities, one might judge that Dandurand was something less than a humble man, and his exaggerated tales of the Flying Frenchmen that he helped personify coincide with such estimations. With much of his legend seemingly self-proclaimed, the tales he helped proliferate about the Canadiens require an inspection in order to differentiate mythology from fact.

Nevertheless, Dandurand was held in high esteem by colleagues and peers. While he certainly did affect great awareness to the exploits of French hockey players, he did not necessarily manage to find too many great French players. Judging by the slim pickings in that area, this was hardly his fault. Yet much of what today's fans know of the hockey club from the Dandurand era come from his many proclamations and bluffs.

Depression, Distractions and Diminishing Assets

While Dandurand was certainly at the Canadiens' helm as the team grew in stature, winning three Stanley Cups on his watch, he was hardly alone in forwarding their cause. As in the case of all winning clubs, a great measure of teamwork and compatibility of personnel was required for the Canadiens to achieve the summit. Coach

Hart, who took over behind the bench in 1926, certainly played an integral role, as did a group of players very much in the prime of their careers. The Canadiens would win back to back Stanley Cups for the first time in their history in 1930 and 1931, with rosters that were largely absent of any francophone vintage. The branding of the mythological Flying Frenchmen continued on deceptively.

The 15 players who contributed to the 1930 championship were Hainsworth, Morenz, Joliat, Lépine, Larochelle, Leduc, Mondou, brothers Sylvio and Georges Mantha, Nick Wasnie, Marty Burke, Bert McCaffrey, Gus Rivers, Gerald Carson and Gord Fraser. The 1930-31 roster of 17 players lost only Carson, while adding Johnny "Black Cat" Gagnon of Chicoutimi; Montreal native Jean Pusie; and welcoming back American-born Art Lesieur. In sum, there were four francophone players on the first championship squad, and an additional two locals for the repeat win. Thus, the club highly touted as the Flying Frenchmen was barely worthy of the distinct moniker that Dandurand had helped brand them. They made up slightly less than one-third of the roster. The Canadiens' great French tradition, twenty years into its existence, had hardly manifested itself by this point, and things were about to go downhill rather quickly. Though the future appeared promising for the Canadiens, fate and the Great Depression had other plans.

At the height of the Canadiens' conquests in the early 1930s, Dandurand and his partners were offered close to $300,000 for their hockey team. Léo, the most active partner in the trio known as the Three Musketeers, declined to sell. Instead, Louis Letourneau, the most silent of the group, opted out, selling his shares to Dandurand and Jos Cattarinich for $150,000. The duo continued on, likely cursing the day they chose to retain the club. Luckily for them, they had proven successful with their racetrack endeavors, which would cushion the blow when they decided to sell the Canadiens in 1935 for a disappointing $165,000.

In the early 1930s, Dandurand and partner Cattarinich, along with ally Lalonde as their coach, envisioned resurrecting the sport of field lacrosse as an indoor game. Calling this seven-man version of the sport "box lacrosse," they entered a Montreal Canadiens franchise into the International Professional Lacrosse League. The proposed six-team circuit, set to be launched at the dawn of the

Great Depression, was perhaps too ambitious in name and concept to have worked at that particular time. NHL owners set to come aboard in Boston, Chicago and New York, joining those in Montreal and Toronto, were hoping to capitalize on the popularity of their hockey clubs. As they sought to play lacrosse in vacant league arenas from June to September, donning the same sweaters as their NHL hockey counterparts, fans began to sense the endeavor as nothing more than a money grab. Newspapers in all cities picked up on the negative public sentiment, and soon the proposed IPLL was down to a four-team Canadian loop featuring the Maroons, the Maple Leafs, the Cornwall Colts and Dandurand's Canadiens.

The owners, jumping the gun, had initially gambled on the potential appeal of a lacrosse league featuring hockey stars adept at both sports, but once it was noted by the press that injuries could, and would, compromise player performance in both sports, the luster of the proposition slammed into a wall. Despite the overall unfeasibility of the proposal, the intriguing concept of bringing lacrosse indoors was decades ahead of its time. Initial curiosity had garnered crowds of five thousand-plus, but after a few contests, the number of lasting loyal patrons settled in at about half that total. Dandurand, Cattarinich and Lalonde's interest in the pursuit would last midway through a third season, the combination of bad press, haphazard planning and inopportune timing dooming it from the get-go.

With the world economy about to spiral, the hockey team slowly veered off the rails following the 1931 championship. The club was aging quickly, with few young and able replacements in sight. After winning a third Cup, Dandurand's interests elsewhere seemed to consume his focus. Hart was also a busy man. When he began coaching in the city, the season lasted 16 to 24 games. A regular NHL campaign now consisted of 44 games, and Hart also had business interests in the city to tend to. To make matters worse, none of the men guiding the club had time to scour the backwoods for hockey talent. It became apparent by the end of the 1932 campaign that the Canadiens were running out of options. Hart feuded with Dandurand during the winter and resigned at the end of the season. Though the Canadiens finished first in the Canadian Division, the odd playoff matchups of the era had them facing the New York Rangers, the leaders in the American Division. When they lost the best of five in four games, it appeared that the Flying Frenchmen who were barely French were heading for their nadir.

As Joliat and Morenz began to show some wear and tear, Hainsworth neared 40 years of age, and the core of four surefire French talents were getting long in the tooth, the Canadiens required an ace or two in order to revive themselves, but all they came up with was deuces. For 1932, only two players were added. Art Alexandre, a left winger from St. Jean, Quebec, would play ten games in this season and only one the next. Defenseman Dunc Munro, born in the United Kingdom, joined after playing seven seasons with the Wanderers. He would retire at season's end.

Habs' great Lalonde was brought behind the bench for the 1932-33 campaign, but his fiery passion could not be transported to ice level. Finishing third, only to lose to the Rangers once more, the Canadiens employed an astounding 22 players in their downward skid. Of the nine players brought aboard, only Léo Bourgault, of Sturgeon Falls, Ontario, made any considerable impact, lasting three seasons. Lalonde was familiar with Bourgault, who had played for him in Saskatoon, Quebec and Ottawa. Seven more players arrived, including journeymen Gizzy Hart and Walter McCartney, from Saskatchewan; Art Giroux from Manitoba; Len Grosvenor and Harold Starr from Ottawa; Leo Murray from Portage La Prairie, Manitoba, and Hugo Harrington from Melrose, Massachusetts.

Typical of the Canadiens' fortune with homegrown talent, there is the curious case of Paul-Marcel Raymond, a then-19-year-old right winger fresh out of the Montreal inner city junior leagues. Raymond had established a reputation as a speedy athlete with the Junior Canadiens team over a pair of seasons, and was often called upon by the Montreal press as an emerging star for the big team well ahead of his arrival in 1932. There was perhaps no single junior player whose mug shot was more prominently featured in the Montreal papers the season prior, but the sleek forward with the slight frame was quite unprepared for the rigors of the much tougher NHL game. His build-up far exceeding his build, Raymond was shuttled back and forth between virtually every Canadiens-sponsored farm club of the time, eventually playing in 76 games over seven seasons, scoring a measly two goals and three assists between 1932 and 1939. Raymond would be the first of dozens of Quebec-bred "can't miss prospects" to meet such a fate.

Approaching 1933-34, there was some hope that trading Hainsworth, the goalkeeper, to Toronto for Montreal-born Lorne Chabot would restore order to the Canadiens' plight, but the move proved to be a holding pattern for the club. Joliat remained at the top of his game, but Morenz had a rough time, scoring only eight times in 31 games. Though the team finished with a winning record, second in their division, it was still quickly ousted by Chicago in the first round of postseason play.

Of the 18 players who would dress for Montreal this season, six were newcomers, with nary a homegrown francophone to be found in the lot. There was Jack Riley, a center born in Berckenla, Ireland, who lasted two seasons. Ontario products included Sam Godin, (Rockland), Jack Portland (Waubaushene) and Adelard Lafrance (Chapleau). Chabot, a local English-speaking product, played all but one game in goal. Wilf Cude, playing on emergency loan from Detroit, filled in for the ailing Chabot. The former NHL rental goalie for hire, Manitoba-raised but born in the United Kingdom, would in the next season become the Canadiens' starting goaltender until 1941-42.

Dandurand Manages His Own Disaster

In January of 1922, as his hockey performance started to decline, Lalonde had become the first Canadiens star to be booed by local crowds. In 1933-34, Newsy watched Morenz suffer the same fate. Dandurand, listening to the crowd's response, reacted similarly, and traded Morenz to Chicago just before the start of the season. In this transaction, however, he would not receive as promising a return.

If the Canadiens' previous season had offered a glimmer of light, the 1934-35 campaign was an outright sign of looming disaster. They finished third once more, suffering their demise during the playoffs at the hands of the Rangers in what was becoming an all too familiar scenario. The number of fans attending Canadiens games in the Montreal Forum could now be counted by fellow spectators, while the city rival Maroons filled the building and were crowned Cup champions at season's end.

Beginning with the dealing of Morenz, Dandurand took on a more active role in managing the team than in years past. Between October and April, the owner made close to twenty trades involving 30 assets, with a half dozen of them being reacquired at different intervals. Coach Lalonde was lost for solutions, feuding with uncommitted players caught in the shuffle. The season began with four successive losses, and the coach took a sick leave after sixteen games, never to return. Dandurand then replaced him on the sidelines, only to witness firsthand what his wheeling and dealing had amounted to. He would promptly sell the club the following off-season.

To illustrate just how poor the organization was in finding suitably skilled players to improve the team, an inconceivable 25 players, including 11 newcomers, dressed for the club over the 44-game season. Teams generally provided sweaters with numerals between one and twenty so fans could more easily identify players, but when the Canadiens broke training camp, Lalonde and Dandurand had difficulty sorting the wheat from the chaff. To help fans recognize those among the unknowns, nine "high numbers" Canadiens sweaters were dusted off from the failed box lacrosse endeavor of a few years earlier to join the others. The employment of unsightly numbers such as 33, 44, 48, 55, 64, 66, 75, 88 and 99 came to epitomize the circus on the ice, with most of the players not knowing which sweater they would pull over their heads until game time. Many of the players, veterans and rookies alike, shared several of these numbers during the course of the season, with Mondou wearing as many as six different sweaters throughout the year. Imagine the folly of fans, not knowing who they were booing!

The mass of players collected by Dandurand in 1934-35 was of strikingly poor quality. Not only were few of them francophone, but also most weren't even skilled enough to last very long in the extremely diluted NHL talent pool. The 11 new players wearing indistinguishable numbers for the Canadiens included such names as Leroy Goldsworthy of Minnesota; Jack McGill of Ottawa; Nels Crutchfield of Knowlton, Quebec; Roger Jenkins from Wisconsin; Tony Savage of Calgary; Joe Lamb from New Brunswick;

Ontario-born Norm Collins (Bradford), Des Roche (Kemptville) and Bob McCulley (Stratford); Polly Drouin of Verdun, Quebec; and Paul Runge of Edmonton.

Drouin, whose given name was Paul-Émile, was perhaps the most successful of the lot. He put in seven seasons with team while drifting back and forth from minor league affiliates. At that, the Canadiens could not even brag of having groomed a local talent from their region. Drouin's hockey apprenticeship, from age sixteen, had taken place in the Ottawa junior and senior city leagues.

Goldsworthy, Jenkins and Crutchfield all arrived as part of the Morenz trade. The key acquisition of the October 1 deal was iconic multi-sport athlete Lionel "Big Train" Conacher, by then an aging 32-year-old superstar rapidly approaching the twilight of his NHL career. A defenseman still capable of delivering thunderous hits, Chicago had been Conacher's fifth and most successful destination after stops with Pittsburgh, Toronto, the Maroons and the Americans. Despite Conacher's reputation as a big drinker, the Black Hawks' Tommy Gorman had taken him on for a season that ended in a Cup win. Despite Dandurand's interest, the Big Train wanted no part of playing for the Canadiens, and after the Habs' manager packaged goalie Chabot and the useful Marty Burke to acquire him, he was quickly informed he would not play for the team.

Enter Gorman once more. Now managing the Maroons, he took the Conacher dilemma off Dandurand's hands with the precision of a skilled surgeon within forty-eight hours. Prior to October 3, Dandurand had acquired the rights to Herb Cain, a large, gutsy left winger, after he was mistakenly left off the Maroons reserve list. With Gorman believing that he had properly secured the player's services, a brief controversy ensued, and NHL President Frank Calder declared Cain the Canadiens' property. The 22-year-old Newmarket, Ontario, prospect had played one season for the Maroons and hoped to remain there. Dandurand now held two assets in his pocket who were not entirely enthused about joining his fading club.

Impatiently, and with no matters pressing, he did not wait for either to solicit better offers in the month leading up to the start of the season. That same day, Gorman offered the Canadiens 22-year-old

McGill Redmen's forward Nels Crutchfield, who had impressed locals in over four seasons of senior hockey in the city, for both Conacher and Cain. Dandurand jumped on it. The two days of trading by Dandurand revealed a classic case study in diminishing assets. In separate deals, he unloaded Morenz, Chabot, Burke, Conacher and Cain for the services of Crutchfield, Leroy Goldsworthy and Roger Jenkins. The latter would play the full season before being dealt to Boston for cash and two further journeymen.

The 28-year-old Goldsworthy, initially acquired on October 1, returned to Chicago in a cash deal 16 days later. Almost one month to the date, Goldsworthy was heading back to the Canadiens for cash once more and was likely left wondering why two clubs who did not appear to want him continued to reacquire his rights. He would play 80 games for the Habs over two seasons, before being packaged with another player and $10,000 cash for star defenseman Babe Siebert and the return of Jenkins.

Dandurand's luck was no better with Crutchfield, deemed the most promising of all assets. After a season of five goals and 10 points, the youngster was involved in a car accident that ended his brief career. Chabot lasted a season with the Black Hawks, while Burke remained for four. As for Morenz, he provided Chicago with some initial spark, only to be traded to the Rangers the following season. He would be returned to the Canadiens for 1936-37, as would Burke come 1939. With Conacher continuing to deliver bone-crunching hits and Cain leading the team with 20 goals, the Maroons won their second Stanley Cup title. Dandurand should have been thanked.

The 1934-35 campaign was the NHL's ninth as a ten-team league. Though the Canadiens had qualified for the playoffs in each of those years, the quality of the league product had been greatly watered down. Fans in Ottawa, long a bastion of support for quality hockey, lost their club when it moved to St. Louis prior to the start of the season. The problem in the nation's capital was that the Senators' faithful had stayed away in droves for most games not involving the two Montreal teams and Toronto. The lesson was a collision of two realities; hockey was now deemed big business, and the fans in the city preferred to spend their hard-earned money during the early Depression years watching players they knew and recognized on local teams from its inner city leagues.

As was the case in Ottawa, there was simply too much hockey in Montreal for fans to support it at every level. The many inner city junior and senior leagues were managing to do alright, with frugal fans paying cheaper prices to admire the efforts of hundreds of French players competing in circuits several rungs below the pro ranks. It was at about this time that it started to become apparent to many that Montreal was either not big enough or wealthy enough to support two professional hockey clubs at once. One of the rivals would have to go, and in most opinions, that team was unlikely to be the 1935 Stanley Cup champions.

Since the early 1930s, Dandurand and Cattarinich were receiving offers from U.S. parties interested in the purchase of the franchise. Dandurand never seriously contemplated selling, and the NHL had made it clear it was not going to approve. What the owners noted, however, was that the value of the offers was in steady decline. Business in the U.S. was not particularly thriving for the NHL at this point. The Philadelphia franchise, which had moved from Pittsburgh, withdrew following the 1934 campaign. St. Louis followed suit in 1935. Cleveland interests continued to beckon for a club, most often targeting the Canadiens, but both Dandurand, who would not see the team leave Montreal, and the NHL would not budge from their stance.

From the end of the season until the league governors meeting in September, not a week passed without rumors printed in the newspapers of an impending sale. On several occasions it had been reported that a sale was finalized, only to be followed by the expected denials. When the owner finally did decide to sell the team in late summer, it was because he had at last worked out an agreement with a consortium of local Montreal investors and businessmen with ties to the hockey community. Dandurand and Cattarinich received a sum reported to be $165,000 and the team would be staying in the city. Given that they acquired the club for $11,000 and had bought out Louis Letourneau along the way for the princely sum of $150,000, the duo's net profit on the sale was desperately slim.

The Canadiens had now existed for a full quarter-century. Despite their ranking in the hockey standing, the franchise had become an iconic staple of the sporting world. This was without a doubt Dandurand's greatest accomplishment and lasting legacy, achieved despite much trial and tribulation. He had forever branded the Flying Frenchmen, regardless of the misconception over the contribution of actual French players. Whether under his watch, or during the Kennedy era, the Canadiens never did find a suitable starting lineup made strictly of local French players capable of measuring up against those of other clubs.

Of the 25 players who wore the Canadiens sweater in 1934-35, only eight were Quebec-born. The starting six were Lépine, Goldsworthy, Joliat, Sylvio Mantha, Jenkins and Cude, of which only two were French-speaking. In 25 seasons, this is how far the plight of French hockey players in the province had come. Had there truly been a Canadiens' "French Player Territorial Rights Rule" over this period, there is precious little evidence that it would have benefitted them given the manner in which the junior and senior city leagues were set up. There were in fact hundreds more French players in the game, but this did nothing to improve the number of top-end quality talent.

If, during the 1934-35 season, the Canadiens' supporters had much difficulty telling the players from one another, they would be just as challenged to figure out exactly who owned the team the following season. The sale was clouded in controversy and the ownership akin to a masquerade.

The worst news of all for Canadiens fans was that this new group would seek in short order to reenact a version of the territorial rights claim that had never helped the club. The owners believed every word of Dandurand's Flying Frenchmen blarney.

2

1935-1940: STUMBLING TOWARD IRRELEVANCE—THE ERNEST SAVARD ERA

A Muddy Transition of Ownership and the Slight Return of the Canadiens' Territorial Rights

Only a mere four seasons removed from its most recent Stanley Cup, the shambles that were the Montreal Canadiens were sold to a trio of Montreal businessmen exuberantly billed as the new "Three Musketeers." The reference to the previous ownership group headed by Léo Dandurand was intended to be flattering. In the Montreal press over the summer of 1935, rumors persisted of an imminent sale, with every wrinkle of innuendo captivating the city's hockey public. Among the more popular threads followed by the papers were stories that involved a sale to St. Louis interests and another that would see the Habs acquired by the owners of the Cleveland Barons. One option, which would not see the hockey club transferred, had to do with the seemingly implausible acquisition of the franchise by the owners of the Montreal Maroons and the Forum—the Canadian Arena Company (CAC). To that end, the biggest questions on everyone's lips were "would the two teams be run by the same ownership, or would they be sinfully merged into one?"

The Maroons and Canadiens had been bitter inner-city rivals since the creation of the former in 1924. Two seasons later, Les Habitants officially moved into the Maroons arena, sharing the home rink owned by the CAC. While the respective ownership groups of both teams had been able to co-exist, their fans were forever at war. As news persisted that the CAC was indeed interested in acquiring the Canadiens, the unusual proposition exploded into full-blown controversy for the fans and press. In the midst of the financial constraints of the Great Depression, the Maroons were Stanley Cup champions while the Canadiens struggled to draw two thousand fans to their games.

The multi-layered controversies gained no clarity whatsoever when the details of the Canadiens' sale were finally made public on September 17. Given the amount of rumor preceding the announcement, the details rendered by the press were viewed with great doses of skepticism. The new owners were a formed syndicate, headed by Ernest Savard, with partners Maurice Forget and Louis Gélinas. There were other unnamed investors in the consortium as well, which opened the deal to even more scrutiny. The trio being well-known Montreal businessmen, the transaction was immediately picked apart by a streetwise hockey public and press. While the men initially denied being tied in any way to the Maroons and the Forum, the public quickly viewed the front men as the "three masked racketeers," operating a veiled charade that barely concealed their association to the men in charge of the CAC.

It was known by the public that the combined resumes of Savard, Forget and Gélinas told of a shared history. They had worked their way up to hockey club ownership as financial advisors, money lenders, property managers and sporting investors. Savard, for one, co-owned interests in the Montreal Royals baseball club. His partner in that enterprise was local lawyer and politician Athanase David, who was also among the CAC movers and shakers. As time passed, the tangle of veiled associations grew more difficult to conceal, until it was eventually revealed in coming seasons that the public's initial suspicions were confirmed. Savard's group was in fact operating as a subsidiary of the CAC.

Nevertheless, upon Savard's acquiring of the club by his syndicate, the initial public statements presented by the group involved an attempt to tactically and cautiously dispel any notion of a potential merger, stating that the Canadiens would proceed as a distinct club from the Maroons. Without going so far as to spell it out, Savard temporarily subdued both the English and French fans with one acute comment on September 22: "I have every intention of giving Montreal a hockey club filled with as many French-Canadians as possible. This will not happen overnight. It will take some time, but we will have a winning club, which is what the public ultimately desires."

Savard also announced that player Sylvio Mantha would coach the team and with that singular gesture showed that there was no evolving plan moving forward. The promise of a more representative French club was the first misstep. Under his reign, he would repatriate former players such as Howie Morenz, a former coach in Cecil Hart, and ask of the NHL a reinstatement of a semblance of the French player territorial rights rule that had never amounted to much privilege for the franchise.

Beginning with the 1935 season, upon Savard's query to the NHL, the Canadiens were granted an updated version of the residence rights wrinkle from 1909 that would ultimately provide them little favor. Consistent with earlier versions, this particular ruling was also not written into the league constitution and was only ever briefly discussed by Savard himself. Explanations of it were vague as well. Initially designated to run for five seasons, the agreement would be extended to seven years, by which time a more specific NHL residence amendment would overrule all preceding versions.

What Savard and the Canadiens were thus allowed was the right to sign players twenty years of age and older, from their region, who were not under any form of pro contract. This meant a free agent, in modern terms, with specific residence conditions attached. They would be allowed to sign two players annually after all pro teams had completed their postseason reserve lists. It is unclear as to whether these two additional players counted or not against the Canadiens reserve list numbers. All told, this special provision was practically useless as it was drawn up. The team would essentially be seeking out the proverbial late bloomers, of which there were few left to be unearthed. They would be left mining for gold in a shaft filled with coal. Savard's granted privilege amounted to little more than window dressing and putting up appearances.

Savard's Cast of Characters Continues the Slide

For 1935-36, the Canadiens would employ more players than they ever had, surpassing even last season's numbers. The new owner's first mistake was appointing himself as manager with no previous experience as a hockey man. In addition, he made team captain Mantha the playing coach. Mantha was on a rapid decline as a player, which would hardly help his command from the bench. Furthermore, players at issue with their bench boss could hardly turn to their captain, who also had a brother on the team. True to Savard's word, he did as promised in increasing the amount of French content on the club, finding a half-dozen francophone players who amounted to little in the long term. The multitudes of minor leagues set up across Canada and the United States now made it easier for Quebec-born players to find work, but they were generally in the minors because they were second-rate.

That logic didn't seem to impart on Savard's choices. He would locate and sign them, give them a few weeks' look, then release or send them back to the minors at will. His first season was conducted as though it was one long drawn out training camp. The 12 returnees from the previous campaign included Aurèle Joliat, Leroy Goldsworthy, Armand Mondou, Johnny Gagnon, Pit Lépine, the Mantha brothers, Wildor Larochelle, Paul Runge, Polly Drouin, Jack McGill and Art Lesieur. All played a regular role on the club. Joining them on the starting roster were goalie Wilf Cude, center Paul Haynes, right winger Joffre Desilets, and defensemen Walter Buswell and Jean Pusie.

Cude was hardly a steadying presence in goal on a team run over by the opposition. Born in the United Kingdom, the 25-year-old acted as a standby for two seasons, waiting to be dispatched to one team or another should their starting goalie fall to injury. He had made his entry into the NHL with the dismal 1930 Philadelphia Quakers, winning 2 of 30 games he played in. When the Quakers folded, he took on the standby position. During the 1931-32 campaign, after two fairly decent performances with Boston, he was called to Chicago to provide a backup for the ailing Charlie Gardiner, then the league's top stopper. Gardiner began the game with a patch over one eye due to an injury he had suffered the game prior. He abandoned fort early in the game after surrendering a pair of goals.

Cude replaced him, allowing three goals in his first twelve minutes of play. Early in the third, he was knocked cold by a Maple Leafs forward, took a few stitches, and returned, letting in six more goals. No teams called upon Cude for all of 1932-33.

In October of 1933, Dandurand purchased Cude's rights from the dormant Philadelphia franchise. He was sent to work in the minors, playing for both the Syracuse Stars and Boston Cubs in two different leagues at once. Making up for lost time, Cude had tended goal six times within eight nights when he got the call to join the Canadiens for the December 23 game against Detroit, subbing for the injured Lorne Chabot. He sparkled in his lone game for the Habs that season, promptly shutting out the first-place Red Wings. Beginning in 1933-34, Cude would become a mainstay in Montreal for four seasons. By the 1940-41 season he was spent. Used sparingly in a backup role by then, his final exit from the Canadiens became a legendary tale. Pondering his hockey fate one day over a steak supper, he declared to all present that his sirloin would decide the matter. "If this doesn't stick, I quit!" he exclaimed, heaving the meat up toward the ceiling. When gravity intervened, Cude yelped, "That's it, I'm done!"

Paul Haynes, a former Maroon and Bruin, was a solid two-way center acquired from Boston by Savard in one of his few progressive moves. Born in Montreal, he would play four solid seasons for the Canadiens and served many more as a scout and coach in their system. A natural athlete, Haynes was both a junior boxing champion and Loyola quarterback before settling on a hockey career. His sharp eye for spotting talent was discovered in 1939 when he was sent to western Canada on a scouting mission which resulted in his finding Elmer Lach and Ken Reardon.

One of the most productive acquisitions at this time was defenseman Walter Buswell, who arrived by way of a multi-player three-way deal with Detroit and Boston. Buswell was a sturdy and dependable rearguard who would miss only four games over the next five seasons. He would be named captain in 1939-40. He was acquired in July on Dandurand's watch, and the deal included the return of the notorious Jean Pusie, hockey's resident on-ice jokester. The entertaining Pusie had a previous stint with the Canadiens, and it was quickly revealed that his skills were terribly flawed. An awkward six-foot-two, 200-pound blue liner, Pusie could deliver a thunderous check. His troubles began when he fancied himself a puck-carrying defenseman. A fast skater, he was cursed with the inability to keep his head up while carrying the puck and was an easily flattened target. Furthermore, he was blessed with a wickedly wild shot that in the words of sports reporter Dick Beddoes was "so inaccurate that it couldn't hit the province of Quebec."

In a journeyman 20-season career that found 28 destination points, it could be said that Pusie wore out welcomes with his combined lack of seriousness and skill. While he was certainly a fan favorite due to his countless antics, his was an act that wore thin too soon for many of his employers. His most notorious moments came two seasons earlier, while playing for the IHL London Tecumsehs. Taking a long pass that turned into a clear breakaway, Pusie blew down the ice and drilled the puck so hard that it brought the goalie's glove right with it into the net. Not about to allow such an odd incident to escape without a show, Pusie retrieved both puck and glove from the goal, waving them in the air for all to see. As fans began to laugh and cheer him on, he grabbed the stunned goalie's hand, counting each finger out loud, making sure they were still attached. He would up this bit of Vaudeville by placing the mitt back on the goalie's hand, patting him on the head as he skated away to delirious applause.

A week later, Pusie was at it again. London was awarded a penalty shot in a game. This was an era in which the coach selected his shooter, and the inevitable chants of "We want Poosee!" came raining from the stands. The coach complied, sending him out. With the spotlight squarely on him, Pusie wasn't about to disappoint his fans and put on a display that became hockey legend in the city. Skating to center ice, he dropped his gloves and stick, pretending to view his victim from afar through a pair of binoculars. Finding the goalie in his mimic, he skated half the distance toward him, stopping at the blue line to shout that he didn't stand a chance. He then retrieved his gloves and stick and took the puck, pondering his next move. After a brief pirouette or two, he kicked ice from his skates and began his descent. Pusie skated in like a whirlwind and spread open for a big windmill windup. Suddenly skidding to a stop, he paralyzed the goalie, freezing himself in mid-swing. He then flubbed a weak, wobbly dribbler at the stunned pad man that skittered through his legs at turtle speed. As if that weren't humiliating enough, Pusie then celebrated gallantly, kissing the goalie on one cheek. As he moved right to kiss the other, the goalie lost it and swung his stick paddle at his head, narrowly missing. He skated back to the bench to the roar of a standing ovation. The following season, Pusie moved his act to the Boston Cubs.

Five other players Savard found played a total of 28 games for the team. They combined for a grand total of two assists and seem only to have been signed to appease the French factor of the team. Gaston Leroux, a 23-year-old forward from the IHL Cleveland Falcons, played two games. He was released soon after the brief trial and joined the Windsor Bulldogs and Springfield Indians. Rodrigue Lorrain was a 21-year-old Buckingham, Quebec, native who had played in the Ottawa junior system. While only appearing in one game, he would make the team the following year and remain until 1942. Montreal-born brothers Conrad and Jean Bourcier were playing professionally with the IHL Pittsburgh Shamrocks when Savard signed them in December. They dressed for six and nine games respectively, with Jean earning a lone assist. It was believed that the brothers were the first two players reserved under the Canadiens new territorial provision. Following their short time with Montreal, they were assigned to the Verdun Maple Leafs. Savard paid dearly for veteran Rosario Couture, who had played seven seasons with the Blackhawks. A francophone from St. Boniface, Manitoba, it cost the owner $2,500 to acquire him from IHL Cleveland. Couture was Providence-bound after playing in only ten games.

Savard lucked out with a pair of players found right in his own backyard. Defenseman Cliff "Red" Goupille was a rock solid, stay-at-home bruiser from Trois-Rivières, Quebec. Goupille was an effective no-nonsense customer, willing to duke it out in abrasive defense of teammates. Though he dressed for only four games late in the season, he would be a welcome commodity on the Canadiens for a full eight seasons. Goupille had been the oldest living Canadien before he passed away in 2005 at age 89.

Perhaps the best acquisition Savard made during his tenure was 23-year-old Hector "Toe" Blake, the second player included in the Chabot deal with the Maroons. Blake, a left winger, had played only sparingly with the Cup champions the year prior but was lighting it up with the Providence Reds when the deal was sealed. He was another discovery of shrewd Maroons hockey man Tommy Gorman, who first spotted him at age 19 starring with the Memorial Cup champion Sudbury Cub Wolves. Blake held his own as a top scoring threat for the Wolves as they moved on to the Allen Cup, a tournament he would also revisit with the Hamilton Tigers in 1934. It was after that second trip that Gorman inked him to contract and he joined the Maroons for their eight final regular season games.

As a youth, Blake sharpened his hockey skills in the mining region near Sudbury known as Victoria Mines. He came about his famous moniker courtesy of a younger sibling who had difficulty pronouncing her big brother's given name. Of medium build in terms of hockey players, Blake was all rock muscle and fiery determination. Having been a member of several successful teams, he owned an ingrained hatred for losing. Blake would light up the Canadiens for thirteen years as a player, followed by another thirteen as coach. His final tally as he walked off into retirement's sunset in 1968 was ten Stanley Cups, two as a player and an inconceivable eight titles as hockey's most gifted mind behind a bench.

On the ice, the Canadiens' first season under the Savard–Mantha duo provided little excitement. Brutal in every imaginable way, they sunk to an abysmal 11-26-11 record and last place in the eight-team league. It became quite evident as the schedule wore on that the Canadiens had few players of any assured value. Bleak as the present felt, the future appeared even dimmer. Apart from Blake, the Canadiens had barely any strong young prospects to move forward with. The experiment with local francophone players had not paid off, on the ice or at the turnstiles. Games had become foregone conclusions played out before 1500 unsatisfied fans. They were gutted by the press in the papers of both languages, with as many articles written about the finances and disorganization as there were about the games themselves. Off the ice and behind the scenes, the once-proud club was also in complete disarray. Since it would take some time in order to restock and stabilize the club, Savard approached a league board meeting, asking for the Canadiens to suspend operations for one season. The request was denied.

Merger Rumors Persist as Clouds Descend

Throughout the season, suspicions continued as to the actual formation of the Canadiens ownership group and of their true intentions. Savard had expressed on multiple occasions that the club was its own unique entity, but his assertions were unconvincing. The absolute lack of transparency by all involved a clouded, simple truth: Savard, Forget and Gelinas did want to own the club in full at some point, but for now, officially divulging that they indeed were tied to the CAC would be a terrible business move. What the public could not entirely be made aware of by this time was that Savard and his partners were in fact subordinates of the CAC to a certain extent, having to report their financial transactions to the corporate bosses.

Prior to their acquisition of the Canadiens from Dandurand and Cattarinich, Savard and his acolytes were each minority shareholders in the CAC. The trio grouped together with close to a dozen additional investors to purchase a majority share in the team. As the syndicate had borrowed from banks and investment firms headed by certain CAC directors, they had essentially made them partners as well, and they remained accountable to these factions financially.

The CAC, with ownership of the Forum and part shares in the Maroons, were hence part owners of the Canadiens as well, by reason of having underwritten the balance of the Savard group's loan. This amounted to a conflicting situation wherein the minority owners in terms of stock, the CAC, had power of approval over decisions by the majority owners who were indebted to them. As with any company, budgets had to be respected, and during the Great Depression when large sums of money were loaned, watchful eyes were kept on every single dime. The initial suspicions of the fans and press were correct, and there were growing fears that the two sides were conspiring to kill off one of the teams to the benefit of the other. Concerns expressed by league sources regarding Montreal being a one-team city fueled the skepticism, and Savard's hockey moves did little to dispel the fans' fears.

A case in point was the St. Louis Eagles dispersal draft of October 15. With the club folding for good, the NHL purchased the rights to the remaining players under contract for $40,000 and charged each NHL franchise a $5,000 fee to participate in the process. Chicago paid their fee, but opted out of the process. The seven-team order of selection was based on a reversal of the previous season's point totals. Choosing first, the New York Americans took forward Pete Cook, which surprised some. The Canadiens were up next and had the choice of four assured values. There was goalie Bill Beveridge, who wouldn't have been an upgrade on Wilf Cude; Carl Voss, leading scorer and former Calder Trophy winner with Detroit two seasons prior; Glen Brydson, second on the Eagles in scoring; and Bill Cowley, a rookie from the Ottawa region and the closest thing to a rising star the league had. Picking second, the Canadiens mysteriously selected Beveridge before trading him to the Maroons that same day for a cash sum believed equal to the amount it cost Savard to take part in the process in the first place. Picking third, the Red Wings reacquired Voss, followed by the Rangers, who grabbed Brydson. Picking fifth, the Maroons added Joe Lamb. Choosing sixth, the Bruins made off like bandits in selecting Bill Cowley. He would win two Stanley Cups and a pair of Hart Trophies with Boston on the way to a point-per-game Hall of Fame career. In all, 18 of 23 players still under contract with the Eagles were chosen, Savard ultimately selecting Irv Frew, Paul Drouin and Henri Lauzon.

Given an opportunity to add an impact player to the club, Savard instead opted to add three low-paid assets to the organization at no cost, and the move did nothing to progress the Canadiens' plight. Additionally, there was no possible way to explain to fans and the press why the Canadiens would choose to select a player with their first pick, only to turn him over to the rival Maroons. The only logical explanation for many onlookers was that the CAC was calling his shots. Publically, the whole of the mess only added more fuel to the fire for those thinking that the Savard group was composed of little more than CAC minions.

The Montreal hockey public was a smart and well-informed group of fans who rarely missed a beat, analyzing and scrutinizing each game and every bit of news that came their way. Their knowledge would have had a lot to do with the amount of press that was covering hockey in the city even then. As many as seven papers of both languages regularly dedicated full pages to the hockey scene. This created a certain measure of competitiveness among the brotherhood of journalists hoping to scoop one another. Several writers had allies in the various hockey organizations in the city and quite often news would emanate in rumor form days and weeks before official announcements. These same journalists could also protect their alliances; the restraint encompassed a multitude of off-the-record subjects, from the players' private lives to the business involvements of the men invested in the hockey organizations. As many newspaper magnates of the time were in fact investors in the hockey business, trust and discretion were high on the list of priorities for most journalists. But not all hockey men on the scene required such white-glove treatment, and not every journalist was willing to alter reality to protect their jobs.

The organizations of the Canadian Arena Company, the Montreal Maroons and the Canadiens were made up of several influential city businessmen, among them bankers, lawyers, financiers, medical professionals, stock brokers, construction and railway magnates and politicians. Brought together under the banner of sportsmanship, they intermingled and meshed well, requiring each other's expertise, influence and money, while also rivaling for positions among the hierarchy. It was power base akin to a spider's tangled web. The press and fans in the city understood that these associated powers were responsible for bringing the game to the public. They followed the evolution of the pro game for twenty-five years and knew that during the Great Depression era, enabling hockey's continued survival could not be the passion of one single wealthy financier. They were aware of which local businessmen were invested, but the francophone majority of the population that supported the Canadiens were becoming increasingly distraught that the wealthy men who made up the directorship of the CAC were primarily English speaking and mostly supportive of the Maroons' interests, if it indeed came down to a matter of choosing which of the two Montreal clubs were to survive. After all, the CAC were owners of the Forum, a fact not lost on the francophone sector.

The Canadian Arena Company partnership was first formed by sportsmen William Northey and Herbert Molson. Northey's sporting interests in the city extended as far back as 1892, when he served as secretary treasurer for the Montreal AAA club that won the first Stanley Cup. Herbert, with his cousin William, was the owner of Molson Brewery. The family also owned the chain of Molson Banks that later merged with the Bank of Montreal. The CAC built Montreal's Westmount Arena in 1989 and Toronto's Arena Gardens in 1912. After the Westmount burned in 1918, the CAC spearheaded plans to build the Montreal Forum and revive the Wanderers franchise as its main tenant. In formulating the project, the CAC took in a wealth of new investors. Donat Raymond, who became a Liberal party Senator in 1926, was front and center among the new parties. He had accumulated great wealth in the hospitality business, owning shares in both the Queens and Windsor Hotels in Montreal. Prior to his appointment to the Senate, friend and business ally Northey convinced him to invest heavily in the CAC's plans, and together they would form the financial conscience of the company. Athanase David, an acclaimed lawyer, businessman and Liberal Party member in the 1920s, followed Raymond's path. He had partnered with Ernest Savard and American baseball executive George Stallings in the successful endeavor of reviving the Montreal Royals ball club and the building of Delormier Stadium in 1928. Other respected businessmen invested in the CAC included James Strachan, president of the Maroons hockey club; Canadiens owner Dandurand, who held minority shares; Dr. David Hart and son Cecil, who had coached the Canadiens; and Ernest Savard, who partnered in the brokerage firm of Savard and Hart with the former coach's family.

Gorman Sticks His Nose In

One person not invested in the CAC was Maroons' manager Tommy Gorman, otherwise known as T.P. Gorman was a newspaper man by trade, but he also happened to be just about the shrewdest hockey mind on the planet. As a youth, Gorman had played hockey and excelled at lacrosse, becoming an Olympic Gold Medalist in 1908. While working as a page boy in the House of Commons, Gorman was recognized for his exuberance and work ethic by the *Ottawa Citizen*, which brought him on board as a junior reporter. Soon, T.P.

graduated from a police column to the paper's sports editor. Not satiated by that rapid climb, he began advising the Senators, in print, on how it ought to be running its hockey club. They hired him as a promotions man, a task he quickly mastered, and within two years he had made his way into the club's hockey brain trust as a talent scout and treasurer. In 1917, an opportunity arose for him to purchase the club in partnership with two Ottawa businessmen. He took a loan of $2,500 from the Canadiens' George Kennedy, repaying him within a year. Not long after the formation of the NHL—a transition Gorman assisted in bringing about—he took on the role of Senators manager. By 1923, he had guided the team to three Stanley Cups.

Gorman was in and out of hockey for a spell when friend and fellow racehorse enthusiast Léo Dandurand called with a favor. The Chicago Black Hawks and owner Major Frederic McLaughlin were in financial straits, and Dandurand had loaned the owner $50,000 to see his way through. The unpredictable McLaughlin was notorious for hiring and firing coaches on a whim. Part of Dandurand's deal would include taking T.P. on as the club's coach and manager. The Hawks were cellar dwellers when Gorman arrived, but in over two years he filled out the roster with veteran skill and had won himself another Stanley Cup. McLaughlin repaid Dandurand, but after a dispute between McLaughlin and Gorman, Gorman resigned. It would have been wise for Dandurand to have hired Gorman for the Canadiens at this point, but he instead recommended that the CAC find work for the brilliant hockey man. They took his sage advice and appointed T.P. as the Maroons' coach and manager. Once Dandurand had gifted him with Lionel Conacher from the Howie Morenz trade, Gorman had all he needed to win a second consecutive Cup. So impressed as they were with Gorman, the CAC then doubled his tasks, making him manager of the Forum. True to his nature, he soon had the building booked solid during both the winter and summer seasons, bringing in everything from senior hockey matches to wrestling bouts and big band performances.

On a more personal level, Gorman could sometimes be a difficult proposition, as he often walked to the beat of a drummer only he heard. T.P. was unafraid to speak his mind when it came to matters involving hockey, financing or politics. From the get-go, this caused an uneasy alliance with the likes of Ernest Savard and Donat

Raymond, as he had little consideration for their respective hockey visions. Matters between the three men came to a head in April 1936, not long after the Canadiens' first season under Savard had ended. Well versed in the intrinsic values of promotion, Gorman let slip details regarding changes being envisioned for the upcoming Canadiens season, six months ahead of the fact.

Privy to a CAC board meeting, Gorman had learned that former coach Cecil Hart was willing to return behind the Canadiens' bench, if the club was willing to reacquire Morenz, then with the Rangers. Likely figuring that such news would heighten interest in the last-place club, Gorman uttered a comment to a reporter, very much on the record. Word was that it was a done deal, and when the inside scoop hit the streets with lightning speed Savard was infuriated. The news sent Canadiens fans reeling at such a prospect, while propelling Savard into denial mode. The Canadiens' owner went so far as to inform Gorman through the press that he ought to mind his own business. Come the following September, once both rumors were borne out, it left Savard looking as though he was hardly in charge of things.

"He Died of a Broken Heart"

On September 1, the Canadiens announced that they had reacquired Morenz in a cash transaction, confirming in the same breath that Coach Hart would make a return behind the bench. Ten days later, a move that would have an even more profound effect on the Canadiens' season was announced. Along with a $10,000 sum, the Habs sent Leroy Goldsworthy and prospect Sammy McManus to Boston for former Maroons stars Babe Siebert and Roger Jenkins. Siebert had scored 83 goals and 157 points in seven seasons with the Canadiens' rival, while forming the lethal "S-Line" with Nels Stewart and Hooley Smith. Although he was now 33 years of age, the experienced Siebert had always played a well-rounded game on both sides of the puck. Hart intuitively converted Siebert into a defenseman, and he produced 28 points in 44 games, earning him the NHL's Most Valuable Player award. Had there been an award for best coach at the time, Hart would also have been a landslide winner. The Canadiens goal differential improved by 45 under his watch and resulted in a first-place Canadian Division finish, one point ahead of the Maroons, and good for second place in the overall NHL standings. After finishing the previous season dead last with a paltry 33 points, the Habs surprised all prognosticators in racking up 54 points.

The incomprehensible turnaround in 1936-37 was attributed to many factors. The return of Morenz had doubtlessly created unforeseen enthusiasm, as he registered twenty points in thirty games. Hart's experienced coaching methods settled both the roster and the individual player roles. Siebert's surprising prominence as a rearguard was part of it, as he often played the full sixty minutes during games. In another light, perhaps it was addition by subtraction that had played a role. Ernest Savard made far fewer transactions as manager in this season, and francophone player trials were virtually inexistent. Despite proclamations prior to the previous season, the Canadiens' francophone content had now been greatly reduced and included only Gagnon, Lépine, Mondou, Drouin and Goupille. Apart from the acquisitions of Morenz, Siebert and Jenkins, only three moves of less consequence were made during the season.

By late January, the Canadiens were a win out of first place, hot off a five-game undefeated run. Prior to a meeting with the Black Hawks on the 28th, Coach Hart was asked by the *Montreal Gazette* for his thoughts on the streak. They wrote that "Hart was particularly enthusiastic about the work of the old line of Morenz, Joliat and Gagnon and of Bill McKenzie's impressive play. The whole team was flying and packing them in wherever they went. A crowd of 12,000 in Toronto on a Tuesday night was something unusual and speaks for itself." The Canadiens had a record of 17-9-3 going into the game, but fate of the worst kind was about to intervene, and the Canadiens would never be quite the same again.

Howie Morenz had been rejuvenated by his return to Montreal. Finding himself on a line with former mates Joliat and Gagnon, the trio had also rediscovered their old chemistry. Early in the first period, Morenz was chasing down a loose puck in Chicago's end, followed closely by Hawks defender Earl Seibert. Just as Howie arrived at the puck, his skate caught a rut in the ice. Seibert slammed into him, sending the star down in a crumple. Those closest to the play later told of hearing bones snap. Morenz had a broken fibula, shattered in four places. His season was doubtlessly over, and it was feared that his career could also be compromised. The team was as destabilized as it had been demoralized, and without Morenz it lost a gear and skidded to a record of 6-9-3 in its final 18 games.

Morenz was taken to St. Luke's Hospital for what doctors told would be a lengthy convalescence. Steel pins were inserted into his leg, which was raised on a weighted pulley that kept him immobile and bedridden for weeks. Morenz kept his spirits up, writing letters to family, friends, fans and well-wishers, assuring them that he was determined to play again. No doubt the most popular player of his time, Morenz always had a constant stream of concerned visitors to his side. Hospital officials became concerned that he was not getting his required rest and proceeded to limit visitors. As time progressed and a more long-term prognosis became clear, it was said that Howie became depressed at the thought of never playing hockey again.

In early March after his father William visited, Howie reported to doctors that he had felt pains in his chest area. Examinations led them to concur that he had suffered a heart attack. His wife Mary and Coach Hart were called by the hospital to be at his side. Before they arrived, late in the night of March 8, Morenz woke and attempted a trip to the washroom. He never made it. Autopsies revealed that a blood clot in his leg had travelled to his heart. His cause of death was listed as a coronary embolism, but perhaps teammate and good friend Joliat put it best when he concluded that his pal, upon realizing that he would never again compete in the game he so much loved, had simply died of a broken heart.

The hockey world mourned the incomprehensible loss of Morenz, a genuinely likable player both on and off the ice. As newspapers announced Morenz's passing to the world the following morning, it was decided that a Canadiens-Maroons game at the Forum that night would go ahead as planned, in Howie's honor. On March 10, a funeral service was held for Morenz inside the same building in which he had so often thrilled fans. Joliat laid a flowered wreath in the form of a number seven on his casket, and an estimated fifty thousand fans passed by it for tear-filled goodbyes. The wake was conducted inside a packed Forum, with patrons paying their respects with silent dismay. The scene was breathtakingly surreal.

Montreal Canadiens' manager Cecil Hart and Aurele Joliat at Howie Morenz's dressing room stall after learning of Morenz' death. *Author: Famous Studio, Montreal*

It would have befitted the Morenz legacy had the Canadiens gone on to win the Stanley Cup, seeing to it that his name be inscribed on the mug for a fourth time. Instead, and logically so, his passing sent the club reeling. In their final five games, the Habs scored only five goals, managing but a win and a tie to show for their distracted effort. Despite the loss of focus, the Canadiens still finished atop the Canadian Division with 54 points, good for second overall in the league. The NHL had continued with its ludicrous playoff format of division winners meeting in the first round, sending the victor directly to the Cup final. The Canadiens measured up favorably against the American Division-leading Red Wings. In six games against the Wings that season, Les Habitants managed four wins and a tie, outscoring them by a 17 to 10 margin. The semi-final began in Detroit on March

23 with a 4-0 loss. Two nights later, the Canadiens were trounced 5-1, and it appeared their season would end in a whimper.

Returning to Montreal for Game Three, Hart attempted some very radical adjustments. Used to shifting his forward lines at four- to six-minute intervals, the coach opted to throw fresh combinations over the boards every two minutes. As the coach proudly noted to a scribe after the game, the Canadiens scored all three of their goals off quick changes, and a new hockey strategy was born. The 3-1 win kept the Canadiens alive, and they closed out the month of March winning by the same score two nights later. Game Four was a different story despite the final tally, as Detroit had matched Hart's tactic move for move, resulting in the balance of scoring chances tilting their way. Had it not been for Cude standing on his head, the series would have wrapped up that evening. Game Five saw Morenz's son, Howie Jr., on the bench for inspiration, and the goalie put in an even stronger performance in the clincher, but the Canadiens ran out of miracles when Hec Kilrea slipped a rebound past the sprawling netminder at the 11:40 mark of triple overtime. While few may have realized it at the time, the loss in sudden death to Detroit would prove to be the high point of Savard's tenure as club owner.

C-Form Slavery and the State of Quebec Hockey

At this juncture in pro hockey's evolution, a standardized form of player contracts became commonplace. With the previously enacted reserve clause of the 1910 NHA, the signing of what became known as the C-Form allowed clubs to retain a player's rights for as long as teams wished for, or until a documented legal release form was given. The "C" stood for confirmation, a legal requisite for persons under the age of 18. Players under that age could sign with parental consent. There were few stipulations to the contract. Players were not entirely made aware that a variation of the contract (the B-Form) could be signed whereby the player only granted the rights to his services should he play in a pro league. Inducing the players to sign the C rather than the B-Form was a fifty-dollar bonus. Signing either document guaranteed nothing. The forms did not include contract terms, which the players bargained for themselves. Not only could clubs extend their hold on players at will via the reserve clause, but they could also release them at any moment without notice. As the hockey agent of today had yet to have invented itself, no player partaking in the practice of signing such contracts would have even considered the deals as being an illegal breach of worker's rights. As long as there were kids dreaming of playing pro hockey, this method was sure to proceed.

Three separate articles in the *Montreal Gazette* of March 31, 1937, perfectly captured the essence of the hockey scene in the city at the time. The pieces combined to show how the game was evolving, where the current situation stood regarding the Maroons, and what loomed on the horizon for junior hockey in the city and province. The first article concerned Hart's new method of changing lines and the ramifications it had on the flow of games. Calling the coach a "quick change artist," the article could not have foretold the pronounced effect this advent would have on the future of hockey. The Maroon article involved team-issued denials that it would be moving to St. Louis at season's end. Pointing to the fact that it had just beaten Boston and was set to make another run at the Stanley Cup, the reports were termed "ridiculous," and claims were made that it had "enjoyed a very successful season financially." However, as the old adage goes, where there is smoke, there is fire. Members of several NHL organizations were in the city and seen at the Canadiens-Red Wings games. They were in fact deciding the fate of the Montreal teams.

The third article was contained in a piece by columnist D. McDonald, and was titled "Junior Hockey in this Province is Neglected." The in-depth piece had been prompted by another poor showing by a Montreal-based club versus Ontario teams in the Memorial Cup playdowns recently held at the Forum. Five paragraphs dissected the consternation, and everything from the methods of producing talent to coaching to league support was brought under question. Teams in the province were not mirroring what had effectively been working in Ontario since the early 1900s. The article attracted much attention in the following days, with many unnamed Quebec hockey men putting in their two cents on the myriad of issues troubling the quality of players and the game in the province. Each opinion pointed a finger at one aspect or another, while never truly finding the gist of the dilemma. The discussions were about the realization that things were not working out and were less concentrated on the potential solutions. Within days, the matters for discussion had spread among many newspapers covering the junior leagues. One solid thought offered was quickly dismissed and involved the local NHL clubs, the Maroons and Canadiens, taking some command of the situation with financial support of leagues and concerted investment into the conscience of a regulatory body. Given the CAC's current troubles and the spending restraint of the Great Depression, it was concluded that it simply wasn't the pro teams' problem to deal with at the time but that the idea had tons of merit.

A One-Team City

In year two of Ernest Savard's career at the helm of the Canadiens, he rolled back his reliance on the French content and the team was successful in relying on players such as Morenz and Gagnon, who were past their primes. In the end, all were pleased with the Canadiens' 1936-37 showing. Management declared that it hoped to pick up where it had left off in the following season.

Following the denials by Maroons management in March that the club was bound for St. Louis, rumors persisted throughout the summer that something was up. These matters were hardly helped by the frequent sightings of Dandurand or Cattarinich in St. Louis, nor were they quieted by the loose chatter seemingly emanating from members of the CAC board. Everyone had a story it seemed, and they all pointed to Montreal becoming a one-team city by season's end. This all might have been decided one season sooner had Maple Leafs owner Conn Smythe not voiced his sentiments. The CAC board, its owners and investors, were all in favor of moving the Canadiens and keeping the Maroons in Montreal. Their logic was simple, but lacking vision. The Maroons, they figured, had recently won the Cup and again had outdistanced the Canadiens in the playoffs. The teams had finished one point apart in the regular season standings, but the Canadiens' balance sheet was not as healthy. Smythe, however, argued that the Canadiens far outdrew the Maroons on the road, with crowds still fancying the old

"Flying Frenchmen" mystique in all U.S. cities. The Toronto owner pointed out that the Maroons drew no better than an average club. His point continued that whatever was healthiest for the league in whole would be best for the CAC and that it would look bad financially if the NHL were to do away with its longest standing member. It was difficult to argue with such logic. What Smythe didn't need to point out to Donat Raymond was the language spoken by the majority of Montrealers.

Dandurand and Cattarinich had a change of heart and wanted to re-enter the hockey scene. They twice offered to purchase the Canadiens from Savard, to no avail. They were left only with the hope that St. Louis investors would be as interested in acquiring the Maroons but encountered indifference as far as that choice went when they visited Missouri. When the NHL's board of governors meetings reconvened in September and the Maroons' fate was decided upon, it settled the question of St. Louis as well. The league decided not to announce the Maroons' fate until after the coming season. The only issue remaining for the CAC was displeasure over not having full ownership of the building's main tenant.

The 1937-38 hockey season was a strange one. The Canadiens, who appeared to be building toward better days, slipped back, finishing fifth in the league with 49 points. They would lose out in the first round once more, this time in a three-game semi-final with the Black Hawks. The Maroons, who had come within one win of participating in a second consecutive Cup final, plummeted to the league's depths with a 30-point showing. Their surprise dive in the standings practically removed all suspense over which club would survive the season. Three key players had all retired, and the Maroons made no effort whatsoever to replace their contribution. They made just one insignificant trade and purchased no players who would spur the team.

The Canadiens, for their part, seemed content with barely treading water. They also made no moves of significance in the signing of seven new players. Though they slipped back in the standings by a mere five points, status quo thinking allowed the Maple Leafs to surpass them and enabled the New York Americans to equal their total. The absence of Morenz spiritually affected the group, as the generally reliable but slowing Joliat seemed lost without him. Coach

Hart pulled stellar performances from the likes of francophone youngsters Drouin and Lorrain, who put in their best seasons in the NHL, as well as old-timers Gagnon, Lépine and Siebert, who were hearing retirement's call. Savard exchanged stalwart defenseman Bill McKenzie to Chicago for the steady Marty Burke, appearing in his third stint with the Canadiens. The lone francophone added by Savard this season would be Quebec-born forward Tony Demers, who appeared in six contests without registering a point. He would last another four seasons with Montreal before achieving infinite notoriety in hockey circles, initially for becoming the first player indefinitely banned from the game for assaulting an official, and later for being the lone Canadiens player ever accused of murder, in the death of his girlfriend. The off-season between the 1938 and 1939 campaigns were marked historically by the demise of the once-proud Montreal Maroons.

Contrary to popular myth, the Maroons did not merge mightily with their one-time rivals, going on to form a dynasty that would alter the course of hockey supremacy. Despite what some misinformed historical accounts suggest, the last-place Maroons auctioned off their most valuable assets league-wide to the highest bidder in order to recoup their losses. The Canadiens managed to afford some leftover bit parts that somehow made them a weaker club the following season. Savard has been historically chastised for his bumbling of multiple Maroon assets at this time, but it was the CAC, not he, which was in control of such decisions. Given his position, his hands were tied when it came to financial matters. If Savard would have wanted to make competitive financial offers for the best Maroons players, he would have required the CAC's approval and money, but he received neither. Now that Montreal had been scaled down to a one-team proposition, it was in the CAC's best interest to own the club that would play in the Forum. The CAC would wrestle the team from Savard in two short seasons.

As it happened, the Maroons finished the 1938 season owning the rights to seventeen NHL players and various minor leaguers and junior prospects. On September 14, Savard snapped up six players. The next day the Maroons sold the contracts of forwards Baldy Northcott, Russ Blinco and Earl Robinson (fifth, sixth, and 11th in scoring, respectively) to Chicago for $30,000. Forward Dave

Trottier was sold to Detroit in December. Goalie Beveridge, defense-men Shields and Croghan, and forwards Shannon and Runge were dispersed to the minors. Center Tom Cook retired. On November 3, Gus Marker, the Maroons' fourth-leading scorer, was sold for $4,000 to the Maple Leafs, where he would post 23-20-43 totals over three seasons. The group of six taken by Savard included the top three scorers in Bob Gracie (12-19-31), Herb Cain (11-19-30) and Jimmy Ward (11-15-26). They also added defensemen Stewart Evans, Cy Wentworth and Des Smith. The Canadiens also took option on three prospects from the Maroons reserve list, goalies Claude Bourque from the Verdun Maple Leafs and Rick Ferley of Winnipeg, as well as Quebec Aces defenseman Lester Brennan.

While it initially appeared that Savard had provided the Canadiens with greater depth, little came of the seven players who eventually dressed for the team. Learning that Gracie would retire at season's end, his rights were sold to Chicago after seven games. Smith put in one solid season on the Canadiens blue line before being sold to Chicago in May. Evans and Ward retired after one season. Wentworth played two seasons for Montreal before calling it quits. Ferley and Brennan never made it to Montreal, but goalie Bourque immediately became the team's starter, appearing in 61 games over two seasons. Cain, playing wing on the second line, was behind Blake on the team's depth chart. He put in a sound campaign with 13-14-27 totals but was traded to Boston in October of '39 for Charlie Sands and Ray Getliffe.

Cain blossomed with the Bruins and soon helped them to the Stanley Cup in 1941. In seven seasons with Boston, he posted 140-119-259 numbers over 314 games. The trade looked particularly one-sided come 1944, when Cain combined with Art Jackson and Bill Cowley (another player who the Canadiens had passed over) to put up 36-46-82 totals. Sands and Getliffe, however, were far from chopped liver. They would play four and six seasons respectively with Montreal, counting for combined totals of 127-155-292 in 378 games. Getliffe would play an integral role on a very tough 1944 club that would finally return the Cup to Montreal. All told, Savard's moving of Cain was far from the worst trade ever made.

If the longtime supporters of hockey in Montreal were bemoaning the fact that the city was now down to one team, no one would have argued had they claimed to have no team at all. The Canadiens got off to a horrendous start in 1938-39, losing its first seven games. A brief streak of three wins allowed Coach Hart a reprieve, but then another skid of fourteen games with only a single win to show did the kindly old coach in. Jules Dugal, a CAC board member who had been an ally of Hart's for years, took over and righted the ship to a 9-6-3 record in its final eighteen games. The Canadiens finished sixth in the seven-team league and lost out in the playoffs to Detroit in three games. If this is what the so-called merger with the Maroons had wrought, many fans wondered why they had bothered to purchase the players in the first place.

It Couldn't Get Any Worse

After Joliat's retirement one season earlier, it would now be Babe Seibert's turn to walk off into the sunset prior to the 1939-40 campaign. While still contributing as the club's best blue liner, he was below standard. Apart from Cain, the Maroon corps did not accomplish much. Young goalie Bourque stole the workload of veteran Cude midway through the campaign, and his play remained average. Savard's Canadiens employed twenty-five players this season, ten of them new to the club. The depths to which the Canadiens had sunk provided a great deal of subject matter for the Montreal dailies. Three points of contention played out regularly in print. In some views, the club had made too many changes to the roster. One grounded opinion claimed that the CAC was not letting Savard do his work, by allowing him to spend serious cash to acquire players in an age where contracts were bought left and right. And then, there were always those who believed that more locals were required to give the team spirit and pride.

All three points were valid ones. Had the Canadiens been able to find a great French player, he might not have instilled pride and spirit in the team all by himself, but he most certainly could have ignited a fire among its francophone supporters. They would have filled the building, and loudly. Stability on any roster is the starting point to success, but beyond an aging core, the Canadiens were having all sorts of trouble finding youthful pieces to relieve them. The dictum of "throwing the torch from failing hands" had yet to enter the Canadiens' sphere. The most troubling aspect affecting the Canadiens' improvement, however, was the handcuffing of Savard by the CAC in order to wrestle control of the team from him.

Up until this time, hockey fans in Montreal had only been privy to the ongoing conflict via speculation presented by the press. The CAC setup with Savard became dysfunctional once the Maroons had been sacrificed. As the present situation had left the CAC without a hockey club they owned outright, a dilemma had been created that would fester until resolved. The fight to gain control of the Canadiens was under way. Savard's plan to that end involved bringing in additional shareholders and giving his group greater combined wealth. With larger operating capital, they could potentially put in a successful bid on the full shares of the hockey club from the CAC. But Northey, Raymond and their cohorts appeared to have no intention of selling. Gorman continued doing a masterful job of keeping the Forum booked, but it appeared as though the income his bookings generated would not be poured into a hockey team the CAC did not own. By restricting the flow to Savard, Raymond and the CAC would be forcing him to sell. It was a battle of wills that would come to a head following one more pitiful season on ice.

Typical of the Canadiens' misfortune in recent years was their search for a coach to replace Hart behind the bench. Dugal did not have the capabilities, and Hart could not be talked into a return. Yet the retirement of the highly respected Babe Siebert, who hoped to remain with the game, offered the Canadiens a potential replacement. Siebert's personal life was a story of sadness. His wife was left paraplegic after the birth of the couple's second daughter. Fans at the Forum routinely witnessed the tough defensemen gently carrying her to and from her seat before and after games. Babe never complained about his lot in life, but his responsibilities were heavy ones. He was held in high esteem by players, and it was thought he would make an excellent coach.

Only a few short weeks after being named to the position, Siebert was vacationing with his family at his father's St. Joseph, Ontario, cottage near Lake Huron. Close to twenty family members, many of them coming from Zurich, were gathered to celebrate the senior Siebert's eightieth birthday. Babe, his two daughters and a family friend had been playing around and swimming near shore when they noticed their inflatable tube had drifted away. With wind picking up, Siebert called his girls to safety and proceeded after the inner tube. Witnesses told that the chase had taken him 150 feet from shore, when he became fatigued and called out for help. A dozen men from the group, fully clothed, ran into the lake after him but arrived too late. Right before them, he sunk down and vanished from their sight. In the next day's editions of the Montreal papers, tributes to the man were numerous. Savard described the tragedy as "a tremendous blow to our club."

Pressed for time, Savard brought in former Hab Pit Lépine, who had just put in a full season of playing-coach duties with the American Hockey League's New Haven Eagles. With a roster of 26 that featured several affiliated players, Lépine had managed no better than a 14-30-10 record. The 1939-40 Canadiens would traffic in an unworkable number of players once again, on their way to what would become the worst season in club history. Looking to avoid the season-opening losing streak of the previous campaign, Lépine got his charges off to a surprising start, going undefeated in the first six games. After 13 contests, their record stood at 7-4-2, and they had outscored the opposition by a 38 to 30 margin. The wheels came off the wagon at that point. Over the next 35 games, Lépine's crew managed but three wins and three ties, as they were outscored 138 to 52. The atmosphere on the club was beyond desolate, with the in-fighting between Savard and the CAC having poisoned any semblance of group spirit.

As the Canadiens' nightmare season was reaching its conclusion, both Ernest Savard and Donat Raymond were at individual crossroads. Savard knew that he could not go on owning the hockey club as things stood. He was in an unworkable relationship with the CAC. With few fans in the seats, there were no profits for their group to put toward the loan they'd used to acquire the club. Raymond, for his part, was tiring of the tussle and briefly considered selling his shares. The headstrong Savard had so far refused to buckle, backed by many fellow investors who felt the same. But now a faction of his allies began to deviate from the unified view. Tired of losing money, they had Savard ask the NHL to suspend the team's operation until the end of World War II. The league wouldn't consider it. Savard, on behalf of his group, approached the CAC with a verbal offer to buy the club outright. It too was shot down. The only recourse left for them was to sell the team.

Louis Létourneau, a former partner in the Three Musketeers ownership, had been brought into the group as an investor. Now acting as Savard's counsel, Létourneau rounded up the group and drafted an official intent to purchase, increasing the previous offer. A second document was also drafted as an intent to sell the team, coming with an affixed price agreed upon by all parties. Both documents contained the signatures of Savard, Forget and Gélinas as well as directors Pierre Rolland, Alphonse Patenaude, Armand Dupuis, John Pritchard, Raoul Grotté, C.N. Moisan, and Frank Commons. In the event of the CAC refusing to sell, the board of directors unilaterally would agree to resign. Raymond and the CAC, to no one's surprise, opted to purchase the Savard group shares, thus putting an end to one of the darkest chapters in Canadiens history.

3

1940-1942: GORMAN BEGINS THE FACE LIFT

Three Visionaries

In the annals of great Montreal Canadiens' managers, Thomas Patrick Gorman's contributions are typically ranked behind those of Frank Selke and Sam Pollock. Due to time's passage and his accomplishments having long been relegated to the history books, the assessment is more than unfair. Gorman took over the reins of a hockey team on the brink of oblivion and turned it into a perennial contender. In six short seasons under Gorman, the Canadiens won two Stanley Cups. Due to the turnaround that he had overseen, the club and players Selke inherited from him were winners. Pollock similarly inherited Selke's body of work.

All three managers, with respect to their distinct eras, mastered different but equally important tasks. Gorman had to find good players, and quickly, in order to revive a floundering franchise. While working for the Canadian Arena Company, he helped foster both the Quebec Senior Hockey League and the Quebec Junior Hockey League by promoting popular Sunday doubleheaders at the Forum. He scouted and signed countless players to C-Forms inside and outside of Quebec, filling out the rosters of junior teams such as the Montreal Royals, the Verdun Maple Leafs and the Montreal Junior Canadiens. The stockpile of talent then moved on to the senior Royals, the New Haven Eagles and the Buffalo Bisons. The system of affiliated teams was a far cry from later, more organized structures of aggregated farm clubs, but it was nonetheless the best Gorman could manage with a restrictive budget. Gorman, in his brief tenure, was responsible for the careers of Canadiens greats such as Toe Blake, Elmer Lach, Ken Reardon, Butch Bouchard, Maurice Richard, Buddy O'Connor, Bill Durnan, Floyd Curry and Gerry McNeil.

Frank Selke's vision comprised part of what Gorman had undertaken. Selke had begun a similar process with the Maple Leafs at the time of his firing, and upon arriving in Montreal managed to convince Senator Raymond and the CAC to bankroll an expensive but profitable system of feeder and seeder clubs that spanned the continent. He established junior affiliations with such teams as the Regina Pats, the St. Boniface Canadiens, the Peterborough Petes and the Hull-Ottawa Canadiens, among others. He continued associations with Quebec-based junior and senior clubs first endeavored by Gorman and sought out many more. Selke put his stamp on the grooming of the players on junior clubs, dividing up the Canadiens' strongest prospects so that they often faced each other on the ice, as opposed to dominating together all on one team. He put the same process in place for the professional clubs Montreal helped subsidize. He employed the coaches on these multitudes of clubs as scouts on the Canadiens payroll, forever on the lookout for young talent. With such a broad net cast and so many players coming under contract, not everyone could be given a chance to make the Canadiens under Selke's watch, but the wealth created by the undertaking stocked a talent pool that was the envy of pro hockey.

Sam Pollock was Selke's understudy for more than a decade. A like-minded hockey connoisseur, Pollock was placed in many roles by Selke, scouting and coaching players and managing teams filled with Canadiens' prospects. He was indoctrinated in the business principles of running a hockey club and taught the intricacies of asset management. By the time Pollock took over from his teacher in 1963, he had 13 seasons of experience under his belt. Pollock was likely the most visionary of all managers once he had taken charge of the Canadiens. He adeptly envisioned hockey's expanded future and began a process in which he sought to maximize the potential of all players owned by the club. Shifting away from Selke's teachings, he allowed players to fulfill their individual potentials on clubs loaded with talent, in order to make them appear much more promising than they were in actuality. Come the 1967 expansion, Pollock would trade many such illusions to teams who would come calling on the Canadiens, desperate for players at all levels. He continued the management of affiliate teams and its associated inventory of talent until the universal player draft made such processes obsolete. He then reaped close to a decade's worth of trickle-down assets from countless player trades stretching well into the mid-1970s.

While the work of Selke and successor Pollock have garnered great acclaim over the years, neither was tasked with Gorman's predicament of turning a pigeon into a phoenix. T.P. Gorman was given little to work with in terms of startup talent. His era at the Canadiens' helm was bookended by the Great Depression and the Second World War. Amidst those constraints, he built the Montreal Canadiens into a winner in just four seasons. He more than deserves to have his name mentioned in the same breath as Selke and Pollock.

Irvin and Gorman Change the Culture

Tom Gorman's résumé by 1940 was quite an impressive one. He had won five Stanley Cups by that time: thrice as coach, manager and part owner of the Ottawa Senators; once as coach and manager of the Chicago Black Hawks in 1934; and again as coach of the Montreal Maroons in 1935. His hockey bona fides were by then beyond doubt. He was also a master of promotion and marketing, well before the term existed. Combined with his background in journalism, Gorman could sell a bicycle to a catfish. Despite the multiple attributes in his portfolio, he would have to prove himself all over again to Senator Donat Raymond and the Canadian Arena Company directors. Gorman's greatest hockey asset was as an evaluator of talent. He was his own best scout, and his track record by then should have spoken for itself. Though he had accomplished more than any of his counterparts, he had to start anew with the Canadiens in Raymond's esteem.

Gorman wasted little time in putting his imprint on his new team, and Coach Dick Irvin spared no sentiment in rounding his group into shape. The Canadiens could not be transformed overnight, both agreed, but it was not unrealistic to hope that they would return to the playoffs.

During the summer, the coach and manager conferred quite often as they went over the club's roster, and the conclusion they arrived at was that they had very little in terms of quality to work with. In September, Gorman visited Senator Raymond to emphasize what depth of change needed to be implemented in order to avoid a repeat performance of the season prior. Yet the Senator felt the club could improve with a few judicious trades. Gorman laughed at this notion and proceeded in no uncertain terms to make his point that the team was a collection of castoffs. He put the entire roster, save Toe Blake, on waivers, with no right to recall. Teams could have any player off the Canadiens' list free of charge. Not a single player was taken.

His point clearly made, Gorman received a budget from the CAC. He would revamp the lineup and bring in any new players that could help. Over a dozen new faces showed for training camp, and Coach Irvin proceeded to run them through the most rigorous set of drills they had ever been subjected to. It was the coach's credo that players were not to get into form during the season. They had to show up in shape at camp, or find it fast. He pushed hard, running them for miles and skating them for hours. Within days of camp opening, Gorman and Irvin could tell without much doubt which men would fall.

Eleven returning players made the grade, including Blake, Getliffe, Demers, Sands, Drouin, Goupille, Mantha, Cude, Trudel, Young and Haynes. Armand Mondou and Cy Wentwoth retired. Mancuso, Summerhill and Thompson were traded by Gorman to minor league clubs for cash. Buswell, Lorrain, Poirier, Raymond and Robinson were cut loose like deuces. While several others remained in the Canadiens organization as minor leaguers, when all was said and done, it was quite the overhaul from one year to the next.

Gorman and Irvin then proceeded, through the course of training camp and during the season, to bring in fresh blood in the form of thirteen new players. They included centers John Quilty, Elmer Lach and Jim O'Neil; forwards Joe Benoit, Murph Chamberlain, John Adams, Stu Smith and Tony Grabovski; defensemen Ken

Reardon, Jack Portland and Alex Singbush; and goalies Paul Bibeault and Bert Gardiner.

Little concession was given by Gorman to sentimentality or linguistic concerns. Players made the cut on merit. There would come a time for more French-Canadian talent on the hockey club, but as it stood, seven Quebec-born players made the roster and the current francophone numbers were reduced to Mantha and Bibeault (Montreal), Drouin (Verdun), Demers (Chambly) and Goupille (Trois-Rivières).

Six significant additions would help the club turn the corner. Haynes is credited with discovering center Lach and defenseman Reardon from last season's scouting mission. Reardon had caught his eye while playing with the Edmonton Roamers, a junior club in the city. Hardly the most fluid skater, Reardon hadn't looked like much of a hockey player until finding his niche as a blue line cannonball. Hitting everything in sight, he threw fear into opponents' eyes with his reckless abandon. That he would make the Canadiens at age 19 spoke for his prowess as a devastating bruiser.

Lach was of an equally fearless breed. The 23-year-old Nokomis, Saskatchewan, native was starring with the senior Moose Jaw Millers and was clearly the classiest talent on the ice. Haynes was impressed with his skillful passing and got his name on a tryout contract. He had previously shunned an invitation to Rangers camp, when advance word came as to how cheap they were when it came to player expenses. He chose not to attend when a letter arrived in the mail telling him to show for camp with his skates sharpened. Released by New York, Elmer then accepted an offer by Toronto to come try out. Barely into his first scrimmage, he was within earshot when Leafs' boss Smythe referred to him as a peanut and figured his chances of making the club were slim. When the owner put $500 in his hands for him and a teammate to enjoy some Niagara Falls night life, the pair used the expense money to return home. Haynes couldn't believe his luck when Toronto removed the nifty pivot from their reserve list.

Much to Haynes's chagrin, however, Lach would also take his position on the club in the first month of the season. The strict Irvin was disappointed with Haynes's effort and production early on. The veteran might have had an eye for talent, but he also had an ear for music. In New York to play the Americans, Haynes skipped a team practice to attend the Metropolitan Opera. Irvin promptly booted Haynes from the team, sending him to New Haven where he finished his career.

True to Gorman's reputation for finding players off the beaten path, he came up with a pair of aces in Joe Benoit and John Quilty. The fact that both players were available to be signed tells much of the era's unsophisticated scouting methods and the apprehensions in regard to assessing talent. Gorman was always a few steps ahead of the competition and was rarely put off by circumstance. He was quite open to travelling distances that others would not go in order to gain a firsthand look at players. It is indeed hard to fathom that club directors of the era were yet inclined to putting much stock into year-end tournaments such as the Allan Cup, the World Championship or the Memorial Cup.

The 20-year-old Quilty was a fresh-faced graduate right out of his native Ottawa's Senior Interscholastic Hockey League, where he had starred with the Glebe Collegiate club. He then joined the Ottawa St. Pats, netting 11 goals in five games during the 1939 Memorial Cup playdowns. Having enlisted in the Royal Canadian Air Force, he had been in training for a year when Gorman signed him to a contract. He would become the Canadiens' first ever Calder Trophy winner, scoring 18 goals and adding 16 assists in 48 games. As would be the case with Benoit, his time with Montreal would be interrupted by military service, though both would return by 1946.

Benoit was a 24-year-old native of St. Albert, Alberta, who had represented Canada as a member of the famed Trail Smoke Eaters club that won the 1939 World Championships. Gorman had taken note of Benoit after he scored six goals in the tournament. His rights were owned by Toronto, who had their eye on a young defenseman in the Canadiens organization named Frank Eddolls. The switch was made in the summer of 1940, and the powder keg would line up beside Blake and Lach to form the first version of the Punch Line. After scoring 66 goals in three seasons with the Canadiens, Benoit was called back to his regiment in Calgary and later dispatched to a smelting plant in British Columbia until the war's end.

Keeping with Irvin's designs on having a more competitive team to play against, Gorman used cash provided by Senator Raymond to add 25-year-old Murph Chamberlain and 28-year-old Jack Portland. Chamberlain came from the Maple Leafs for $7,500, and Portland was a known quantity to Montreal. A rugged defenseman with a penchant for bone-jarring hits, Portland had been sold to Boston in 1934 for a sum of $7,500. It cost Gorman an additional five grand to bring him back this time.

When Irvin was first announced as coach of the team, he promised little in terms of improvement. All that he would commit to was his word that the Canadiens would make the playoffs. In a seven-team NHL, that meant no less than finishing sixth or higher. Irvin was not shooting for the moon. After finishing dead last, sixth place was the least of improvements. To that notion, Montreal won six more games than it had the season prior. They finished sixth, one point behind Chicago. They then met the Blackhawks in a best of three series. All games would be decided by one goal, with the Canadiens winning Game Two on Forum ice to force a third game, which they lost. Consolation was found in the merest of improvements. There was nowhere to go but up.

A Slow Climb Back Uphill

The Canadiens won two more games in 1941-42, finishing sixth with a record of 18-27-3. The Habs' 39-point showing was just a one-point improvement on the previous season. Their playoff script was an exact replica of the previous campaign, only this time they were outdone by Detroit, losing on the road while winning at the Forum in the three-game set.

Gorman and Irvin made modest adjustments to the roster for the season. Ken Reardon's brother Terry joined the club on loan from Boston for one season while his passport troubles were worked out. The addition of the center was a crucial move coming three days after Lach went down to injury and was declared out for the season. Typical of Coach Irvin's traits, he promoted the hard-working Emile "Butch" Bouchard to the club, although his skating at the time left much to be desired. Strong as a bull and fearless, Butch endeared himself to the coach by showing an exemplary work ethic and a strong willingness to improve. When Irvin learned that Bouchard biked 40 miles from St. Hyacinthe into camp each day, he knew he could turn the industrious 21-year-old into a valuable commodity.

A judicious move was made early in the season by Gorman when he signed an entire line from the Montreal Royals to help with the team's floundering offense. With only a win and a tie to show for the first dozen games, he brought up Buddy O'Connor, Gerry Heffernan and Pete Morin, better known as the Razzle Dazzle line. While the trio did not remain intact for the entire season, the addition had a pronounced effect. Over the final 36 games, the Canadiens' record was 17-17-2, good enough to match their sixth-place showing for 1940-41.

The task for the Canadiens and Gorman in 1942-43 would be to maintain, or even improve upon, their status as a .500 hockey club. Once more, Gorman's ability to find players in a pinch served the team well. With Ken Reardon off to serve in the war and Red Goupille injured six games into the season, Glen Harmon was called up from the Junior Canadiens. Gorman found Harmon out west, where he played in two consecutive Memorial Cups with the Brandon Elks and Winnipeg Rangers. He would stick with the Canadiens for a full nine seasons. Offensively, Montreal was immediately improved by Lach's return to full form, his 18 goals and 40 assists being second on the club. Gorman also spent a whopping wad of cash, $30,000 to be exact, in purchasing Gordie Drillon from the Maple Leafs. Drillon scored 28 goals that season but departed for the war as soon as the season was over, never to play again. Luckily for the Canadiens, they did find a winger to replace Drillon in young Maurice Richard, who had shown great promise in training camp.

The 1942-43 Canadiens finished with a 19-19-12 record, despite a tumultuous first-half showing. After winning three of their first four games, they then went on a long skid, winning just three of their next 17 games. At the midway mark, they had garnered just 19 points in 25 games, but they turned it around in the second half, going 12-6-7 down the stretch. Overall, the fifty-point finish was a sizeable improvement over the previous season.

The Canadiens were slowly rounding into a very good club, but few would have predicted them to lose only 13 games over the next two regular seasons combined. With the war capable of ravaging a club's roster in any given year, Gorman and Irvin could only expect them to continue improving. The 11 ties were one concern, as were the many games in which the club was blown right out of opposing rinks by dauntingly high scores. The thinking was that if the Canadiens could solve their goaltending issues, they may be able to contend for the Cup.

In a few short years, Gorman had built a powerhouse. The Canadiens would finish first in each of the next four seasons.

4

WARTIME MYTH

Rocket of War

"He's just a wartime hockey player," was a quote made famous by Toronto Maple Leafs general manager Frank Selke in the mid-1940s, shortly after Maurice "Rocket" Richard scored 50 goals in as many games in 1944-45. With NHL teams having contributed many players to the cause, the general consensus was that the hockey product was greatly watered down by the loss of enlisted players.

While the assumption regarding Richard went unchallenged at the time, the notion that he was simply a wartime hockey phenomenon took root and gained ground in the hockey world. After the war ended and many of those same players returned, Canadiens Coach Dick Irvin Sr. offered a rebuttal: "Well the war must still be ongoing, because Richard is still scoring."

While the Rocket never again enjoyed the torrid 50-goal pace he set in 1944-45, he did top the 40-goal mark in three of the following six seasons. The reasons for this apparent drop in production take nothing away from his accomplishment. After Richard set the mark, he became the target of opponents. It was clear teams needed to focus on Richard in order to defeat Montreal. In addition, from the end of the 1946 season to the beginning of the 1949-50 campaign, the schedule increased by twenty games. The longer season contributed to the players becoming more fatigued as the season wore on. The grueling pace also led to more injuries, and Richard was no exception. Finally, the players returning from the war, including a pair of first-rate goaltenders, played a part in reduced scoring league-wide.

Nonetheless, the Rocket's scoring feats were practically given an asterisk by Selke's initial comments. Once Selke had moved his managerial talents to the Canadiens' front office in 1946, the "wartime" perception was rarely put forth by him ever again. For the next 11 seasons, the Rocket would finish among the League's top five goal scorers. Despite this, the wartime hockey player tag remained attached to Richard's feat in the minds of many.

Since 1945, the plateau of 50 goals over 50 games has been equaled seven times by four different players who accomplished the task from the beginning of the season to their club's fiftieth game. On five other occasions, players reached the total in as many games, but they did so beyond their club's fiftieth game played. In all these instances, the leagues were greatly watered down in comparison to the era in which Richard played.

Conn Smythe's Propaganda

Once Richard proved to be more than just a wartime aberration, Maple Leafs owner Conn Smythe began to propagandize that the entire Canadiens team of this era was essentially composed of wartime cheaters. It was much in Smythe's vein to take digs, founded or not, at his French-Canadian rivals, and he often claimed that he did this to motivate his club in games against them.

Smythe had also held onto lingering sentiments over the conscription crisis of World War I, wherein relatively few francophone men enlisted compared to those from the rest of Canada. Having served in both World Wars, he often found issue with the Canadian government and their methods of enlistment and front line training. When the Second World War broke in 1939, many Canadians readily volunteered, but conscription this time around was not put into effect until 1944. In his position as captain of the Canadian Officers Training Corps, he had harsh criticism in the newspapers for the practices involving the Quebec-based regimens. Several of them had been deployed overseas, such as the Royal 22nd Regimen, the 12th Armoured Regimen and the Mount Royal Fusiliers, but they were never stationed to fight alongside the English-speaking troops due to language training issues. Consistent with his sentiments regarding enrollment during WWI, Smythe still felt that not enough men from Quebec were signing up when in fact volunteer and conscription numbers in the province were way up in comparison to 1917. Hockey players on the whole, due to being among the last to enlist due to their profession, simply weren't the preferred warriors for battlefield assignment. This was an inconvenient truth for Smythe and others who saw the players' duties extending to the front lines.

In *The Paradox of Conn Smythe: Hockey, Memory and the Second World War* by J. Andrew Ross, the writer begins his expose on the Leafs' owner during wartime by detailing the findings of a 1951 article in Canadian weekly *Saturday Night*. Ross writes that the magazine characterized his refusal to condemn "the lagging patriotism of his players" while at the same time putting his own life on the line as "the psychological paradox of Conn," and concluded that he was simply selfish and blindly loyal to "anything which he himself has created or developed."

Other authors have been less kind. Fabled hockey writer Trent Frayne once wrote of Smythe that he "was a bombastic, romantic, bigoted, inventive, intimidating, terrible tempered paradox of outlandish proportions." Frayne's wife, June Callwood, added that he was "a high-hearted despot who had learned to simplify the confusion of his childhood by eliminating the soft baggage of tact, tolerance, forgiveness and sociality by which most people draw closer to one another." Journalist Ralph Allen, a friend and ally of Smythe's offered perhaps the most succinct portrayal when stating that the Leafs' owner was "as diplomatic as a runaway rhinoceros."

While serving in World War II, Smythe in his dual roles as both a hockey man and a Major, regularly traversed the ocean, going back and forth between Canadian and European soil. At home, he would often be quoted in a tangle of army duty and hockey-related predicaments. More than once, his Maple Leafs had been heavily scrutinized for failing to contribute many players to the war cause. Smythe, harangued by these accusations, dismissed the charges as being ridiculous, noting how the majority of his players were enlisted and ready to serve when called upon. That they weren't already serving was the crux of several editorialists' claims.

This troubled Smythe, as it exposed the duality of several of his actions. Several photo ops featuring Leafs' players had been contrived and published in newspapers, purporting to show their commitment. All during the course of previous discussions he had regarding the preparation of Canadian soldiers for war, Smythe had made grand-standing proclamations on several related matters. Combined with the player photos, this had brought him positive attention. With the habits of the Maple Leafs players' war regimens then exposed, the accolades were now being pulled back. With fingers now pointed squarely at him for the Maple Leafs' practices, he deflected the negativity by pointing out how the Canadiens were essentially doing the same thing. In loudly repeating such claims in the Toronto press through his multitude of newspaper allies, the stain of cheating the war effort was then hung onto the Montreal team. For many minds in English Canada, the Smythe spin stuck, but anyone closely examining the Canadiens roster would note that it had been affected as any other in the league when it came to losing players to the war effort.

The critiques about NHL players' participation were commonplace from many news outlets. In 1942, the league published a list of 77 players on seven teams serving with the Army or the Royal Canadian Air Force in order to appease the sentiment that players had some sort of free pass. The Canadiens players, on T.P. Gorman and Donat Raymond's orders, were all told to contribute and find work in some fashion, which they did.

Leonard Peto was a director on the board of the Canadian Arena Company and the president of the Montreal Royals hockey club that had become the Canadiens' primary senior affiliate by the early 1940s. Peto was also the vice-president and managing director at the Canadian Car and Foundry Company when it was turned into a munitions plant during the war. In his capacities, he found work for all Canadiens players exempt from service for one reason or another. Despite public perception, or Smythe's accusations, most hockey players, when given the choice, wished to enlist. They were sometimes prevented from doing so for lack of a high school diploma, injuries sustained or their age. Anyone who owned a business or operated a farm was also exempt.

Manager Gorman bristled at the notion that the Canadiens players were not part of the effort. As he was quoted in several Montreal newspapers, "The day of the tourist hockey player is definitely out as far as the Canadiens are concerned. Hockey is most definitely of a secondary consideration to the bigger job of winning the war." Before running off the names of players committed in the effort, Gorman noted that he was doing so only "because there has been some criticism of the part being played by professional hockey players."

The list of Canadiens involved was impressive: Ken Reardon was in battle overseas; Bunny Dame and Joe Benoit were stationed at a smelting plant in Trail, B.C.; Toe Blake worked summers at a munitions plant in Hamilton; Charlie Sands worked at a shipyard in Fort William; Jack Adams, John Acheson, Marcel Dheere, Bill Fraser, Grant Hall, Herman Gruhn, Gordie Poirier, John Quilty, Ken Reardon and Pat Tracy were all in the R.C.A.F. Terry Reardon, who was refused entry in the service due to color-blindness; Maurice Richard; Elmer Lach; Jack Portland; Pete Morin; Gerry Heffernan; Buddy O'Connor and Jimmy Haggarty worked year-round at Peto's plant. Paul Bibeault was studying for a position in the Army Commission. Ray Getliffe, who owned a shoe store in Stratford, was taking military training. Butch Bouchard and Red Goupille, both farm owners, were exempt.

Richard attempted to enlist on three occasions but was turned down by the military each time. In 1939, at age 18, he was refused because he hadn't completed high school. He had left before receiving his diploma to work as a machinist in order to help his family make ends meet. He took courses, and upon graduation two years later, he attempted to enlist once more. By this time, he had accumulated several injuries while playing junior hockey. He was declared unfit, as X-rays showed that he had suffered a broken ankle and that his femur and wrist had not properly healed. He then applied a third time, as a machinist, but he was refused for not having a technical trade certificate. Richard then took a four-year course at a Montreal technical institute, but by the time he received his certificate the war was over.

Canadiens as Hard Hit as Any During World War II

NHL team rosters were most affected by player enlistment during the 1943-44 season. Several teams lost core elements that year, and when the season ended the Canadiens were greatly criticized for allegedly sacrificing less talent than other teams by comparison.

Around the NHL, the impact of war on team rosters was severe. The most famously affected was the Boston Bruins team, which lost the services of the entire "Kraut Line" of Woody Dumart, Milt Schmidt and Bobby Bauer following the 1941-42 season. That year the trio had accounted for a total of 41 of the club's 160 goals and the Bruins finished third in the standings with 56 points, four back of the league-leading Rangers. In 1942-43, minus the Kraut Line, the Bruins finished second, four points behind the leading Red Wings. They scored a whopping 195 goals, an increase of 35 in absence of their top line. While many believe the loss of the Krauts was the most impactful change, what actually hurt the Bruins most was losing goaltender Frank Brimsek to the Coast Guard for two seasons starting in 1943-44. That season, Bruin players would tally 223 goals, while surrendering a dreadful 268. Bert Gardiner, a 30-year-old goalie who had his NHL career extended because of the war, was far from an able replacement.

In New York, the Rangers also sacrificed a top trio to the war effort, with brothers Mac and Neil Colville, flanked by Alex Shibicky, missing in NHL action starting in the 1942-43 season. In 1941-42, the line's last season together, the trio accounted for 42 goals. New York went from 171 goals scored down to 161 the following season, perhaps a less than expected decline considering the circumstances. Yet due to the efforts of Phil Watson, Bryan Hextall and Lynn Patrick, who combined to score 63 times, the offensive numbers were not as low as some might have predicted. What hurt the Rangers most was the loss of 21-year-old rookie goalie "Sugar" Jim Henry to the service. Without Henry, the Rangers' goals against ballooned from 143 to 253 in a single season. In Henry's absence, the Rangers record dropped from 29-7-2 to 11-31-8. The following season, the Rangers employed a horrifying 34 players, while grounding themselves to a 6-39-5 record. In the two years, the Rangers had tried six different goalies, but none were capable of stopping the flood.

The Detroit Red Wings were most fortunate during this time, as they lost few young stars to enlistment due to owning a veteran-heavy roster. After losing the Cup in seven games to Toronto in 1942, they went from fifth to first place; a nineteen-point improvement that resulted in the franchise's third Stanley Cup. In 1943-44, the Red Wings would drop to 58 points, still good for second in the

Montreal Canadiens hockey team, October 1942. Back row (left to right): Portland, Lee, Bibault, Laforce, Goupille, Richard, Bouchard. Front row (left to right): Carragher, Harmon, O'Connor, Heffernan, Lach, Demers, Adams. *Image available from Library and Archives Canada under the reproduction reference number PA-108357.*

standings. Over this time the team core consisting of Syd Howe, Don Grosso, Mud Bruneteau, Carl Liscombe, Joe Carveth and Adam Brown remained intact. Along the way, Detroit would add Harry Watson and Murray Armstrong to their roster but would lose the valuable Sid Abel for two seasons.

The standing of the Chicago Black Hawks, a perennial bottom feeder in these times, was mostly unaffected by enlistment. From 1940 to 1945, Chicago finished either fourth or fifth in the league. Brothers Max and Doug Bentley were the Hawks' leaders by 1944, the elder Doug leading the NHL in goals and points for 1943. Max would depart for service first, missing two seasons starting in 1944. Doug would join him one year later, with both returning in 1946. During their departure, their roles were ably filled by Clint Smith and Bill Mosienko.

Toronto was not as affected by the loss of enlisted players as were the Bruins and Rangers. Though they did lose a significant number of players, the Maple Leafs were better prepared than most in filling roster spots when players departed. Of 19 players on the 1942 club, only eight returned the following season. For 1943, there were an incredible 16 new faces in Toronto's lineup. One year later, the Leafs had 12 returnees and 11 new players. Depth was certainly the key for Toronto.

Following their 1942 Cup win, the Leafs lost top scorers Sweeney Schriner and Pete Langelle and traded leading scorer Gordie Drillon to Montreal. Still their goals scored increased by forty the following season. Gaye Stewart, George Kennedy and offensive rearguard Babe Pratt helped compensate for the departures. Goaltender Turk Broda and top scorer Syl Apps were each among the best at their positions in this era, and Toronto lost both for the '44 campaign. Despite the loss of Apps, the addition of Rookie of the Year Gus Bodnar kept the goal scoring up, as the Leafs scored sixteen more goals that season. The Leafs' goaltending chores were split between veteran Paul Bibeault and 35-year-old former Toronto and New York standby Benny Grant. Implausible as it may seem, the pair allowed only fifteen goals more than Broda had in 1943. Between 1940 and 1945, the Leafs finished the regular season either second or third. Four enlisted players returned from service to rejoin Toronto for 1945, and with the addition of goalie Frank McCool the Leafs won another Cup.

It is curious to note that while all of Toronto, Boston, New York, Detroit and Chicago had lost star offensive players during the period of 1942 to 1945, their goal scoring generally increased from season to season. The lone exception was the Rangers, who had gradual decreases each season, dropping from 177 to 154 over that period. Interestingly, in 1945, Toronto scored 31 goals less the previous season and still won the Cup. The addition of McCool in goal accounted for 13 less goals against.

So what of Richard, the "wartime hockey player" and his band of "cheaters" in all this?

First of all, it needs to be dispelled that Richard's goal total in 1945 was any kind of fluke. While the Rocket's feat constitutes an anomaly or an aberration of sorts, it could not be due to the so-called watering down of the NHL product at the time.

For three consecutive seasons during the Second World War, scoring increased among NHL teams. As a note to accuracy, it should be stated that the 1940-41 and 1941-42 seasons were two games shorter, and for the purpose of following trends, the total for the Brooklyn Americans teams have been removed. In 1940-41, the teams that would come to be known as the Original Six counted 801 goals. In 1941-42, five of six teams increased their individual totals for a league-wide increase of 113. The Bruins were the lone dissenter, dropping from 168 to 160 goals. A similar augmentation occurred for 1942-43, with an additional 179 goals scored league-wide. This time it was the Rangers dropping by 16 goals to 161. For 1943-44, the six NHL teams reached a total of 1225 goals, 132 more than the season prior. Chicago scored one goal less than the year before.

Historians would point to the 1943-44 season as the peak for "wartime hockey players." The season was indeed an aberration, as nine different players topped the 30-goal mark. It was unforeseen. The players included Chicago's Doug Bentley (38) and Bill Mosienko (32); Boston's Herb Cain (36) and Bill Cowley (30); Toronto's Lorne Carr (36); Detroit's Carl Liscombe (36), Mud Bruneteau (35) and Syd Howe (32); and Montreal's Richard (32). For all of these players, except the Rocket, these numbers would represent career highs in goals. As for these players hitting the 30-goal plateau in other years, Bentley, who had scored 33 the season prior, would be called into service in 1944-45, never coming near the mark upon his return. Cain would drop down to 32 in 1944-45 and Mosienko would finally reach 31 in 1951-52, when seasons were expanded to 70 games. Richard would exceed 30 goals on seven different occasions.

The NHL's upward scoring trend stopped for the 1945 campaign, dropping by 82 goals from the previous season. The games were becoming tighter. Players in the service were slowly returning to the game, and scores were down due to three solid new goaltenders having established themselves on the scene. Seven of the nine 30-goal scorers from the previous season all scored less in '44-45, apart from Maurice Richard.

How the Rocket Punched 50

The achievement of scoring 50 goals in 50 games by the Rocket went against all scoring trends of the time. How and why it happened as it did was difficult to explain or analyze. The fact the feat was not accomplished again by Richard or any player for another 36 seasons testifies to the perfect storm of elements required to allow something of that nature to happen. In 1943-44, the NHL adopted the center ice red line to eliminate two-line passing and limit offside calls, thereby speeding up the game. While it did result in increased scoring that season, total goals scored dropped in 1945 when Richard's numbers went up.

The NHL game was certainly destabilized by players leaving to join the service. It affected all clubs and all players left to compete. Where it was most obvious was in the quality of the goaltending, which was uncharacteristically poor for a few seasons. Richard was among a number of players who had a career year in 1943-44, and though the others did not increase their numbers the next season, the Rocket might have had an advantage or two that others did not.

For the 1944-45 campaign, the players starting to return from the war and the new goalies coming into the league knew very little of Richard. He was 23 years old starting his third season, but due to injuries he had only played in 71 regular season and playoff contests. For many, he was still very much an unknown quantity. In the season and a half Richard had played up until that time, his linemates varied depending on who was injured.

During the 1940-41 season, a right winger named Tony Demers found some temporary chemistry playing on a line with the slick and sleek Elmer Lach and the rugged Toe Blake to their left. A photo running in several newspapers of the day shows them christened as the "Punch Line." There is also a popular photo of Richard posed to the left of Demers and Lach. A later variation of the line featured Joe Benoit in the place of Demers. Up until this time, Richard had rarely played to the right of Lach and Blake for more than the odd shift or two. The Rocket was a natural right winger. He had played the right side all his life. But with the Canadiens in his first two seasons, Richard had always been employed by Coach Irvin on the left wing due to his left-handed shot. Players of this era simply did not play on their off wing. Sticks were always pointed toward the boards for defensive purposes because that was how opposing defensemen were positioned. Left-handed defensemen played the left side and were used to seeing nothing but right-handed right wingers. It was what they dealt with game in and game out.

With a little less than 20 games remaining in the 1944 season, Irvin began to experiment with his lines. He was having trouble finding a suitable replacement for Benoit alongside Blake and Lach. On February 12, with 16 games remaining in the season, he decided to give Richard a shot at the position during a game in Toronto. Richard produced two goals in a 3-2 win, and the more legendary version of The Punch Line was born.

Opposing defensemen had a hell of a time defending against the player not yet known as the Rocket. He would bear down on them, eyes filled with fury, making the expected cut toward the side boards. In the instant that the defender would go for it, Richard cut toward the middle, with all kinds of free space between himself and the goalie. On the next shift, Richard would deke toward the middle, and then take the outside lane, catching the defender off step, before curling in behind him. The more Richard shifted his approach in the offensive zone, the more he gave defenders fits. What he instinctively sought to achieve was to put a defender in a backhand position to his forehand. When all else failed, the Rocket would just fireball straight at them and bowl them over.

With Lach and Blake, he'd found perfect linemates. It could also be said that they had found the perfect foil. Once Richard was united with them, he started on a goal per game pace, scoring 19 in the final 16 games of 1943-44. He'd add 12 more in nine playoff games, on the way to the Canadiens' first Stanley Cup since 1931. After scoring 50 in 50 games in 1944-45, he added six more goals in as many playoff games. All told, Richard did not merely score 50 goals in 50 games; he had scored 87 goals in 81 games. Not bad for a player initially deemed by his own coach to be "too brittle" to last very long in the NHL.

Richard's injury history up until the end of the 1943 campaign had been very concerning to the Canadiens' organization. As a junior, he had broken his right ankle and suffered wrist and shoulder injuries the following season. He had been signed by Canadiens GM Tommy Gorman following a 133-goal season as a 17-year-old in the Quebec Amateur Hockey Association system. From there, he graduated to the Montreal affiliated Verdun Maple Leafs junior club and then to the Senior Canadiens club of the QSHL. He had not played 40 games at either level by the time he tried out for and made the Canadiens in 1942. After 16 games, Richard hadn't looked out of place, but then he broke his left ankle, prompting the Irvin quote. The Canadiens offered his services to the five other clubs, but found only middling interest in the player. Toronto was curious enough to ask what the Canadiens would expect in return and the Rangers were interested but balked at trading forward Phil Watson. It seemed as if Richard was motivated not only by Irvin's words, but also the fact that no team thought him good enough. His response is in the record books.

Gorman's Shrewd Moves Pay Off

For 1942-43, the NHL decided to limit rosters to 15 players per team. It was the standard then that clubs would dress nine or ten forwards, four or five defensemen and a goalie. Because of injuries and wartime commitments, Montreal employed 27 players that season. They finished with a 19-19-12 record, the first time they had achieved a .500 standing since the passing of Howie Morenz in 1937. The war had decimated their roster for 1943-44, but it actually helped the club select the players it could best use. Several of the players employed by the team the previous season had destination restrictions placed on them by the service. Some were allowed to play only home dates, while others could remain inside Canada and make trips to Toronto. Looking at 1943-44, the Canadiens chose only players that were able to cross into the United States. The rulings actually helped the lineup coalesce.

That would be an advantage to them, as only eight players of twenty-seven from the previous season played with the Canadiens in '43-44. The Canadiens had lost some good ones by this time. All-Star defenseman Ken Reardon left after the '42 season and they would now be deprived of the services of Joe Benoit and Gordie Drillon, who combined to contribute 58 goals in 1942-43. The eight returning were Maurice Richard, Toe Blake, Elmer Lach, Butch Bouchard, Buddy O'Connor, Léo Lamoureux, Ray Getliffe, and Glen Harmon, and they were joined by nine mostly newcomers to form a roster of 15 and two spares that would make it through the season without major injuries.

Two players were known quantities. Gerry Heffernan, who had a good first year with the Canadiens in '41-42, had been returned to the Royals thanks to Gorman's efforts to have his travel restrictions removed. Murph Chamberlain returned, after being on loan to Boston for a season. Fern Majeau was brought up from the Senior Canadiens squad and Bob Filion graduated from the Royals to fulltime duty. Twenty-nine-year-old defenseman Mike McMahon of the Quebec Aces, known for his pugilistic skills, was signed as a free agent. Tod Campeau and Bobby Walton were spares from affiliated clubs used in two and four games respectively. The remaining two acquisitions by Gorman fell into hockey lore. Both were shrewd maneuvers that had gotten Conn Smythe's goat.

Phil Watson was a local francophone product who had been starring with Rangers for eight seasons. The Canadiens had their eye on him for quite some time and had tried more than once to acquire him. When all else failed, Gorman sprang into action. According to legend, the Rangers star, who had enlisted, somehow had travel restrictions placed on him quite mysteriously for the 1944 season, preventing him from playing in the United States. Watson spent off-seasons in Montreal working at the Fairchild Aircraft plant and was required to work a certain number of hours per year. It seems Watson was not meeting the quota, hence the restriction. Fingers pointed quickly toward Gorman, as he was all over it, working out trade details with Lester Patrick, the Rangers GM.

On October 26, Patrick announced the stipulations of the deal. Watson was to be loaned to Montreal for one season for the services of Ditch Hiller and Charlie Sands. There were also future considerations and further stipulations. While Watson could not play outside Canada until meeting his hours quota, he would then be allowed, pending a second trade with Montreal, to play against all U.S. clubs apart from the Rangers. By December 9, Watson had put in enough overtime at the plant to qualify, and the Canadiens complied by sending Tony Mahaffy and Fern Gauthier to New York. Eleven days later, Gorman had the Rangers game clause lifted when he traded unused Tony Demers to the Rangers. Watson was now permitted to play anywhere and ended up appearing in 44 games, contributing 49 points. Coming from the Rangers' top line, he provided the Canadiens' second unit with higher than usual skill. At the end of the season, all six players were returned to their respective organizations.

Curiously, the deal confirmed that day also played into the legend of Rocket Richard. The Canadiens were playing an exhibition game against the Bruins one hour east of Montreal, at the Cornwall Community Arena. They had been exiled from the Forum as the Army had taken over the building for the offseason. Just as they had done with a game in the same building one season prior, all proceeds from the match were destined for the Canadian Red Cross. The Rocket must have liked the Cornwall Arena. Almost a year to the day, on October 22, 1942, he had scored his first-ever goal in a Canadiens sweater in Cornwall against the Bruins. He signed his first Canadiens contract seven days later. This time around, the Rocket did even better, treating Cornwallites to his first-ever hat trick as a Canadien. The Rocket was very inspired that evening. Earlier inside the arena, he had been informed about the birth of his first child, a daughter weighing nine pounds that he and his wife would name Hugette. As Charlie Sands, who wore number nine, had just been traded to the Rangers, Gorman offered Richard the number for the game. After the hat trick in Cornwall, the number would never be worn by another Canadien.

The other great move by Gorman prior to the 1943-44 season fell into his lap strictly by happenstance and serendipity. It only took some underhanded coercion by Gorman to make it all fall into place. The Montreal Royals signed goaltender Bill Durnan in 1940, but the Toronto native had not come to Montreal in pursuit of furthering his hockey career. Durnan had in fact soured on thoughts of playing professional hockey following his contractual release from the Maple Leafs one year earlier. The Leafs had ruthlessly cut him loose after Durnan had shown up for camp with an injury. Gorman had scouted the goalie, as he helped the Kirkland Lake Blue Devils to the 1940 Allan Cup championship. Gorman soon learned that the primary concern in the young man's life was finding career work, with playing hockey as a secondary matter. He then put Durnan in contact with Len Peto, who offered him both a position with the Canadian Car and Foundry Company, and a job as the Royals' goaltender.

As far as puck stoppers go, Durnan was more unique than any other in the long and celebrated history of his distinct brethren. Goalies have always been different personalities. Durnan set himself apart as the only ambidextrous goalie in hockey history. Naturally right-handed, he began a practice in his youth of wearing catching mitts on both hands and switching his goal stick from side to side depending on the shooter's angle. The tactic stymied opponents, and in three seasons with the Royals he was quite the sensation. But unwilling to sacrifice the income from his day job, he refused to consider turning pro. He enjoyed the stability of earning a working wage at the plant combined with the added income from senior hockey. At age 27, he figured pro hockey to be a foregone conclusion he could not commit to full time.

Starting the 1943-44 season, the Canadiens were in a bind. Gorman was opposed to going back with Paul Bibeault in goal and Bert Gardiner was too old for the rigors of the NHL. Their best prospect had been Bill "Legs" Fraser, who was now committed full-time to the service. It was Durnan or nothing, and Gorman needed to find a way to entice the netminder into signing with the Canadiens. He offered a fairly decent salary for the time, and then increased the sum to $4,200 per season. Still Durnan balked. The standoff continued until moments before the Canadiens' first game on October 30. After undergoing some pressure from Peto, Durnan signed, quickly got dressed in his equipment and went out to face the Bruins. The game ended in a 2-2 tie.

Durnan and the Canadiens did not lose a game until a 5-4 loss in Boston on December 2. So sensational was Durnan in backing the Habs, he did not lose a single game at the Forum all season. The team finished with a 23-0-2 record at home and a 15-5-5 record on the road. He finished the season conceding only 109 goals in 50 games, for an average of 2.18. At season's end, Durnan was awarded the first of his six career Vézina trophies. He was perhaps the biggest reason the Canadiens turned their fortunes around.

The 1944 Canadiens destroyed all competition on their way to the franchise's fifth Stanley Cup. After losing the first playoff contest to Toronto on March 21, the Habs responded with a 5-1 win two nights later. Richard scored all five goals and was awarded all three stars for that contest. Montreal did not lose the rest of the way, with Rocket tallying 12 goals in total and the frugal Durnan surrendering 14 goals in nine games.

Considering he could have had all of Lach, Richard and Durnan on his team, it is little wonder that Conn Smythe was upset. Though the Canadiens would win it all again in 1946, Smythe's discourse rarely deviated from the norm. He would continue to slag Richard, the "wartime" hockey player and the "cheaters" he belonged to. In years to come, the Leafs owner would spout even more absurd propaganda, directed at the notion that the Habs were hoarding all the best French-Canadian players when his Maple Leafs did not dress a single French-speaking player for 25 seasons.

During wartime, heroes were looked up to by the public and rarely questioned. In the Toronto region, Conn Smythe seemed to do no wrong. He had founded its hockey club, built Maple Leafs Gardens right in the middle of the Great Depression, and gone to war for his country twice. All were commendable achievements attributed to a strong, confident personality. A war hero and a great Canadian, few were prepared to dispute his loaded verbal persuasions and convictions. Smythe's bold pronouncements on hockey matters became gospel. Often attacking the Canadiens and French-Canadians in the same breath, he displayed his truest nature when in Montreal for various political or sporting functions. Addressing the local gatherings, he would open with: "Ladies and Gentleman . . . and Frenchmen!"

Ironically, by 1947 Smythe wanted the Rocket on his Toronto club and made a cash offer of $75,000 to the Canadiens for his services. Smythe had found an old Richard photo, as a junior dressed in the blue and white uniform of the Verdun Maple Leafs. In a primitive nod to photo-shopping images, he had a graphic artist superimpose the Toronto name above the Verdun letters, making a prospective sale seem all the more imminent. Both the photo and the offer were laughed at by the Canadiens' brass. Montreal would get used to having the last laugh.

The Toronto–Montreal dichotomy grew even deeper in the summer of 1946, caused once more by a Smythe repercussion that came back to kick him. While Smythe was involved with war matters and stationed overseas, he had appointed his trustworthy assistant Frank Selke to manage the club in his absence. A trade completed by Smythe in 1940 and later undone by Selke caused friction between the pair, leading to their eventual split in 1946. Smythe had acquired defenseman Frank Eddolls from the Canadiens in 1940. Not only had the youngster shown a great deal of promise as a junior, but also the player was enlisted in the RCAF. During wartime having such types of players made Smythe look good for a spell. Contrarily, when Selke traded Eddolls back to the Canadiens in 1943 for budding star George Kennedy without consulting Smythe, it made the Leafs' owner look bad. Kennedy then went on to become one of the greatest Maple Leafs of all time.

Smythe complained loudly about the Eddolls deal. Certain members of the Leafs' board of directors thought Selke should be the club's General Manager, but upon the termination of the war, Smythe returned to his functions as full-time GM and he relegated Selke's role to diminishing proportions. Much to Smythe's despair, Selke promptly quit, taking his hockey talents to the Canadiens' front office, replacing Gorman starting in 1946-47. Under Selke, the Habs would win five Stanley Cups in succession from 1956 to 1960.

The last laugh, indeed!

5

1942-1967: MISCONCEPTIONS OF THE CANADIENS "FRENCH PLAYER TERRITORIAL RIGHTS RULE"—PART 2

The Tangled Web of the Norris Hockey League

The 25 NHL seasons from 1942-43 to 1966-67 fondly known as the Original Six Era comprised professional hockey's most restrictive and retentive period. Though it is considered by those who lived and breathed the game then to be hockey's highest peak, the league was a virtual entertainment monopoly run by a handful of wealthy business magnates. Throughout the quarter century, the owners did little to broaden the popularity of the game. They resisted expansion and the potential dilution of their product; they were weary that television would hamper ticket sales; they buckled down on player salary increases and conspired during labor unrest to withstand player unions. It was also the era in which three of the six NHL teams won twenty-four of twenty-five Stanley Cups.

The Original Six nickname is a misnomer that came after the fact. When the league doubled its size in 1967, the moniker was used in reference to the more established clubs, who for three seasons would form the NHL's East Division. Prior to 1942, the NHL had as many as ten teams going back to the 1930-31 campaign. When the NHL was originated in 1917-18, it comprised four clubs. The era was restrictive and monopolistic for other reasons. The ownership of franchises rarely changed hands. In Boston, the Bruins' owner from its inception in 1924 until 1972 was grocery tycoon Charles Adams and his family. The Boston Garden, originally known as the Boston Madison Square Garden, had been built and designed by Tex Rickard, the original owner of the New York Rangers. Grain and railway magnate James E. Norris acquired the Detroit Red Wings in 1932 after attempts to purchase both the Rangers and Blackhawks failed. His family held onto the club until selling to Mike Illitch in 1982. When the Chicago Blackhawks' original owner, coffee tycoon Major Frederic McLaughlin passed in 1944, the franchise was taken over by a syndicate run by club president Bill Tobin, whose primary backers in the purchase were Norris and realtor and banking magnate William Wirtz. James E. Norris owned the largest shares in the Madison Square Garden Corporation, owners of the Rangers. Norris also owned Chicago Stadium, where the club run by Tobin and Wirtz were his tenants.

In Montreal, the Canadian Arena Company ran both the Forum and the Canadiens until selling to the Molson family in 1957. Maple Leafs Gardens, and the team it was named after, was run by majority owner Conn Smythe, who began divesting his shares in the early 1960s to a group that included his son Stafford. Smythe often liked to joke, albeit sarcastically, that NHL stood for the Norris Hockey League. The Norris' influenced balance of power was in place by the dawn of the Original Six Era, and Smythe's unveiled gripes suggested that the American clubs seemed to always get their way, voting in unison when it came to matters of league policy.

Homegrown Allure

From the time that professional hockey became popular in the early 1900s, there has always been an allure for the homegrown player. This was true of all sports, no matter the region, and such thinking continues to exist to this day. The ticket-buying public swelled in great numbers whenever a local talent starred with a local team. To that end, NHL club owners in 1942 sought to protect their right to such players and came up with a version of a territorial rights clause that in league history had only ever been granted to the Canadiens in 1909.

Franchise owners had wanted to institute such a clause for quite some time, but with two teams in Montreal until 1938 and another two teams in New York up until 1942, it remained an impractical vision. When the Brooklyn Americans hockey club folded prior to the 1942-43 season, the window for such a clause opened wide.

In hindsight, one may wonder why the American-based clubs would agree to pass such a ruling that would seem unfavorable to them. Had they been against the ruling, they would have vetoed it, en bloc. In the context of the day, however, it was looked at much differently. From the perspective of U.S. team owners, there seemed to be a growth in both the number and quality of American-born players starting in the 1920s. There were amateur clubs with American rosters winning national championships, and the U.S. Olympic hockey teams were seen to be doing well on international stages. They had won silver medals in all Olympic Games they had participated in from 1920 to 1956.

As the hockey Olympians remained amateurs, they could only play in exhibition games against NHL teams. Because they trained harder as a unit than most NHL teams, they often gave the pro clubs all they could handle. By 1942, there had been 14 players from Massachusetts play in the NHL. Some such as Carl Voss, Mickey Roach and Lou Trudel were quite good. The state of Minnesota had produced close to 20 NHL players by this time, including goalies Frank Brimsek and Mike Karakas, and forwards Cully Dalhstrom, Doc Romnes and Leroy Goldsworthy. New York had an amateur team known as the Rovers that played at MSG that was drawing quite well. The owners figured the day wasn't far off when there would be an influx of American talent to their teams.

With the mindset that there could one day be greater players to be found within their territories, the American team owners were intrigued by a homegrown player clause that would protect their own interests. Even if the player did not come from their own backyards, there was always a way to market and profit from an All-American athlete.

In 1942, the NHL brought in the fifty-mile radius ruling that gave each of the six teams a virtual protected zone that would allow them the exclusive right to sign players to C-Forms up until age 20. The

American owners were not the least bit concerned about this ruling giving the teams in Canada an unfair advantage. There were several ways to acquire players and many areas in which to find them.

The Players Came From All Parts

The method in which organizations accrued talent and managed the total count of their contracted players had similarities with the practices in place in hockey today. Apart from NHL rosters, teams had signed prospects playing on their minor affiliates and junior clubs. Reserve lists dictated how many players a team could own, and each season they were required to release players in order to make room for newer ones. If a team found a player who was under contract to another club but somehow left off that team's reserve list, he could hence be placed on their reserve list. If a player had been given his release, he became a free agent. Teams had negotiation lists on which they could place the names of as many as four players, regardless of age, provided that he had not been signed by another professional club. Players had no say in whether they could be placed on this list or not. If a desired player was signed to a pro contract by a minor league team, NHL clubs could purchase that player's rights at any time.

In addition to all this, during the span of the 25 Original Six seasons, the NHL held annual drafts to help teams acquire better players. Prior to the beginning of each season, teams sent their NHL player reserve lists to the League's head office. All players left off the lists could then be acquired for a fee in what was called the Intra-League Draft. If a team selected a player, it had the choice of whether to place him on its reserve list. If the team put the player on reserve, it was then required to drop a player. The NHL was also involved in a similar process with the American Hockey League clubs in what was called the Inter-League Draft. In these transactions, the AHL clubs listed players for NHL teams to select, generally for a nominal fee if a player transaction could not be worked out. An opposite process called the Reverse Draft then followed for the benefit of the AHL clubs. The Inter and Intra League Drafts had been going on long before they were given their names and the results were disclosed in newspapers. Prior to 1957, the papers simply reported the transactions and cash sales as regular trades.

There are others reason why the four American teams were not concerned about the effects of the radius ruling. In the six seasons between 1937 and 1942, five different clubs won the Stanley Cup. There were no dominant teams. In fact, there were also five different Cup winners from 1932 to 1936. There was a great balance of power in the NHL; Toronto had won in '32 and '42; the Rangers won in '33 and '40; the Black Hawks won in '34 and '38; the Red Wings won in '36 and '37; and the Bruins won in '39 and '41. The lone Cup won by Montreal in these eleven seasons was claimed by the Maroons in 1935, and they no longer existed. While the Canadiens had preoccupied themselves with finding French players no one else wanted with which to fill their rosters, their rivals surpassed the club that had won back to back Cups to begin the '30s. They did this by finding players everywhere but in Quebec.

When the fifty-mile radius ruling era began in 1942, the only concern would have been the southern Ontario region, which owned the greatest concentration of players in the country making it to the NHL and had long been the providence of the Maple Leafs. Like all clubs, Toronto could only have so many players contracted to them. Such concerns would have been whiffed away with the back of a hand. In Quebec, or the Montreal region specifically, the concentration of players by population was likely higher, but quality was deceptively poor. Not only were the Canadiens not winning with francophone players, no other teams were as well.

The 1941 Cup-winning Bruins were largely from Ontario. They dressed 19 players that season, 13 of whom were from southwestern Ontario. The remaining six came from Manitoba (2), the Maritimes (2), Quebec (1) and Minnesota (1). Conversely, the Cup-winning Leafs of '42 had ten players from the Canadian Prairies, eight from Ontario and one from New Brunswick.

The Sad State of Organized Hockey in Quebec

Judging a hockey player based primarily on where he is born, where he is trained and what language he speaks can involve conflicting appraisals. When it came to assessing Ontario-born players versus the Quebec-born players by the 1940s, the general consensus was that quality tilted greatly in favor of the Leafs' region and the territory previously occupied by the Ottawa Senators. The reasons were quite simple. Since 1890, amateur hockey in the province of Ontario came under the purview of the OHL, which structured and ruled over all junior and senior associations. The OHL had set standards from the onset, and since their rule was province-wide, they banished clubs which failed to adhere to their regulations. The standards covered a myriad of aspects, from coaching and training to game rules and basic eligibility requirements.

The Quebec Amateur Hockey Association was founded almost 30 years later in 1919 and was initially comprised of a half-dozen teams near Montreal. The snag in all this was that Quebec had hundreds of teams aligned in dozens of badly run local associations not bound to any higher authority. Like the OHL, the QAHA was tied to the Canadian Amateur Hockey Association. The QAHA's rulings, teachings and guidelines were never as stringent, in that they allowed themselves to play for provincial titles against clubs that were not associated under their banner, nor that of the CAHA. For that reason, numerous hockey associations in the province never had the impetus to join the QAHA, thus their players never received grooming of equal quality. Well beyond 1919, the teams in the various Quebec hockey associations remained under no specific governing body. This would explain why, in coming years, scouts stayed away in droves. Evaluating a hockey player from Quebec was akin to spinning a roulette wheel. A series of future Quebec junior leagues and associations were better at conforming over time, but the late start still affects the QMJHL today.

Beyond this, there was another reason why Quebec-based players were shunned for the most part. The scouts of the day were far from scientific. They knew of the language of the province, but most couldn't speak it. They held similar apprehensions over whether players speaking minimal English could take instruction from coaches and managers who did not speak their mother tongue. It had little to do with prejudice at first and had much more to do with compatibility. Evidence of this remains in today's NHL, wherein teams draft Russians, Swedes, Czechs and Finns only after assuring themselves that they will mix in well. Similarly, the hockey clubs of the Original Six era weren't all that intrigued by French players from Quebec when they could find players of an equal or better level of play elsewhere.

Prior to 1942, only five Montreal Canadiens players who were truly francophone would in time become inducted into the Hockey Hall of Fame. They were Didier Pitre, Jack Laviolette, Georges Vézina, Joe Malone and Sylvio Mantha. Equally, francophone players of quality were not in great prominence in the NHL one year prior to the advent of the territorial rights ruling.

During the 1941-42 season, 157 different players suited up for the seven NHL teams. Of those, 144 were born in Canada; nine in the United States; three in the United Kingdom and one in Russia. The Canadians by province of birth were as follows: 55 from Ontario; 28 from Saskatchewan; 27 from Manitoba; 14 each from Alberta and Quebec; four from New Brunswick and one each from Nova Scotia and British Columbia. The largest contingent of Ontario players were on the Bruins and Red Wings, with 17 and 15 respectively. The Cup-champion Toronto Maple Leafs had eight.

The Montreal Canadiens in 1941-42 dressed a total of 27 players, of which nine were born in the province of Quebec. Four of them were born in Montreal (Buddy O'Connor, Gerry Heffernan, Emile Bouchard and Paul Bibeault); two more were born nearby; Pete Morin (Lachine), and Tony Demers (Chambly); another two (Murph Chamberlain of Shawville and Rod Lorrain of Buckingham) came from north of the Outaouais River near to Ottawa; and Red Goupille, who was born well north of Montreal, in Trois-Rivières.

On the other six NHL rosters that season, there were a total of five Quebec-born players. They were Phil Watson of the Rangers, Jimmy Orlando of the Red Wings and Ken Mosdell of the Americans. All were all born in Montreal. The Bruins' Bill Cowley was from Bristol, northwest of Ottawa, while Fred Thurier came from Granby, southwest of Montreal.

Watson, the lone francophone of the five, had played for St. Francis Xavier of the Montreal City Junior Hockey League, later joining the Montreal Royals of the QJHL. The Canadiens failed to sign Watson to a C-Form. He thought himself better than their meager offers and held out for more. He signed a $4,000 per season contract with the Rangers in October of 1935.

Mosdell had played as a junior with the Montreal Royals when he was signed to a contract by the Brooklyn Americans in October of 1941. He would later make it to the Canadiens, where he would play for 14 seasons. Orlando, a tough customer, was a late starter in junior hockey, joining the Montreal Victorias of the Montreal Metro Junior Hockey League at age 22. He would spend six seasons in various Montreal inner city leagues before signing with Detroit in 1938. Thurier had played for the Canadiens farm club of the same name in the Quebec Senior Hockey League in 1936-37.

The American owners dreaming of homegrown talents were going to continue filling their rosters with Ontario boys and Prairie stock. Quebec would remain an afterthought.

The Dark Horse Phoenix

From all appearances, no one involved with hockey in 1942 could have predicted that it would be the Montreal Canadiens, of all teams, who would come to rise to supremacy in the Original Six Era. The lone reason they made the playoffs at all was the existence of the perennially dismal Brooklyn Americans below them and the seven-team format that allowed six teams a chance in the post season. There were certainly no precedents to indicate that the Habs would find a method to work the fifty-mile territorial rights rule to their benefit. But that is exactly what they managed to do.

Contrary to popular perception and myth, the course taken by the Canadiens was not one the team itself had plotted out for their ultimate gain. The situation was one imposed upon them by the territorial radius ruling, which came to benefit them in numerous ways. In part, it had something to do with players in the province of Quebec cropping up latently, due to the QAHA's tardy arrival as a governing body. The 1919 establishment of the QAHA framework, mainly in the Montreal region, only now began paying dividends a few seasons into the Original Six Era. The team was also about to benefit from the first generation of locally born players who grew up as Canadiens fans. Players in their late teens and early twenties had surely learned a thing or two from Morenz, Joliat and company, and the two Cups won at the start of the Great Depression.

History had so far revealed that Tommy Gorman and Frank Selke were the smartest, shrewdest and hardest working of all hockey thinkers. Without ever having worked together with the Canadiens, their visions coalesced. Gorman had started a process to enable a better system of junior clubs for the Canadiens, and Selke took that ball and ran with it. Proverbially speaking, that same ball would one day be handed off to Sam Pollock, who would learn of moves and maneuverings known to no previous student.

Gorman's efforts proved to be just one of a number of things to come to fruition to impact the Canadiens' growth. Between the time of the Maroons' demise and the Habs' resurgence, he was charged by the CAC to manage the Forum. Ever the taskmaster, Gorman had filled the building with junior and senior league matches that not only drew large crowds, but also heightened the profiles and expectations of the players. The framework of highly competitive junior league games helped school the previously undisciplined players into the greater conscience of teamwork. What the QAHA struggled to regulate over twenty years, Gorman happened upon by implementing a simple form of showcase struc-ture. Once the radius rule came into prominence and the play-ers learned of its existence, it heightened the stakes even more. In essence, the structure that the QAHA itself alone could never impose got a kick in the pants with the application of the radius rule. The thousands of Quebec kids playing hockey and wandering in the wilderness now had a compass.

It is doubtful that the incentive provided by the radius rule could, on its own, transform the pitiful state in which hockey found itself province-wide. For the multitudes of Quebec youths who felt they might never get a shot at the big leagues, further inspiration came with the Canadiens Stanley Cup of 1944 and the Rocket's fifty goals the following season. The hero Richard became to hundreds of thousands of fans can never be underestimated. On his shoul-ders, he would carry their dreams. He was soon idolized, his ges-tures emulated and his persona adored. When he became known as The Rocket, the French attempted to brand him with a fran-cophone nickname. When "La Comète" failed to catch on, they began calling him "Monsieur Hockey," a moniker that stuck until his retirement.

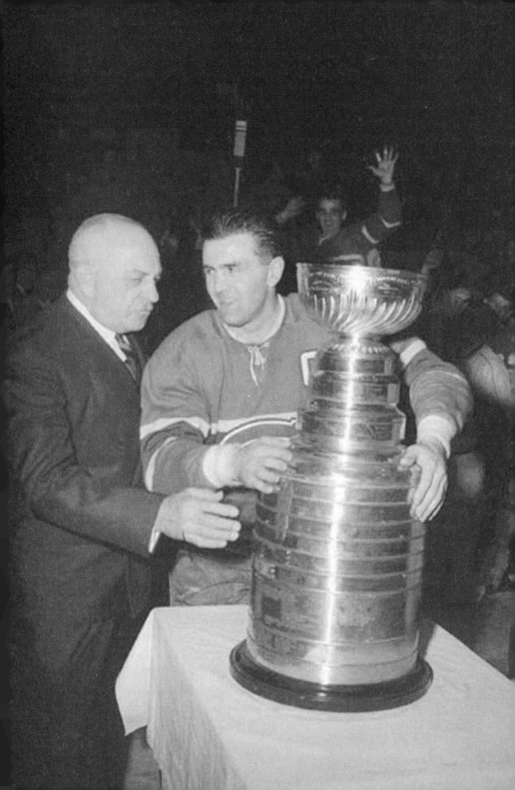

What Richard inspired among Quebec hockey players was the realization that Average Joe could make it big. The Rocket did not skate smoothly, nor did he pass the puck with silky skill or play in his own zone with great measures of defensive accountability. What he did do better than everyone else was take the puck and drive to the goal, almost willing pucks deep into the net by his sheer single-minded determination and perseverance. He brought an unforeseen passion to his work. Though Richard was unique beyond description, that notion did not prevent the masses from seeing themselves in him.

Richard's effect on the Quebec hockey populace cannot be discounted. If Gorman's simplistic setting of the stage played into the creation of a greater awareness, and the NHL's establishing of the radius rule opened a window, it was indeed the Rocket's influence which pushed players to exceed themselves.

What most hockey historians with an anti-Canadiens bias have failed to note is that Richard became property of the team well before the territorial radius rule was enacted.

Selke's Tricks of the Trade

Tom Gorman and Senator Donat Raymond had an adversarial relationship to many extents, and there have been accounts that tell of the CAC head being untrustworthy of the manager's willingness to spend money to improve the club. When Gorman left the organization in 1946 and was replaced by Frank Selke, Raymond not only gave the former Leafs' manager carte blanche to refurbish the Forum's decrepit appearance, but he also provided him with the budget to completely overhaul the Canadiens' system of farm clubs and minor affiliates. Not only was Selke well versed with finding players all throughout Ontario, but he was also well connected

Maurice "Rocket" Richard and Fred "Cyclone" Taylor with Stanley Cup in Montreal; photographer unknown (April 16, 1957)

Source: Library and Archives Canada/Library and Archives Canada/Gazette collection/PA-132397

with every neck of the woods out west. Most importantly of all, he had worked alongside Dick Irvin for years and was extremely familiar with the type of player the coach was able to get the most out of. Such philosophical synchronicity was a serendipitous blessing.

It has been reported that the Canadiens, at the peak of their powers, spent upwards of $300,000 annually on their sponsorship program of affiliated clubs. The investment would have incurred everything from the salaries of players, the contracts and related expenses of scouts, coaches and other minions, and travel and moving expenditures. The more the Canadiens made, the more that was put back into the process.

Both Selke and Irvin were avid breeders of a wide variety of chicken and rare fowl. They'd raised them in all sorts of regions under different situations. Due to neighborhood complaints, Selke once had the local police running through the backyards in Cote St. Antoine, searching for his noisy Partridge Wyandottes. Through a multitude of similar livestock experiments, Selke began to note how the birds reacted to the conditions. Some were better off raised and groomed in certain regions than they were in others. He translated his theories to hockey players, establishing a succession of minor league affiliates in the United States, which would evolve from year to year, and junior teams in Canada that were near the regions where the players were raised. He then groomed the players with two notions in mind: placing them in situations where they would excel and in situations where they could be challenged.

Depending upon the particular circumstances of a player's grooming, they were moved about based on their individual challenges as players. Similarly, if an affiliate team had a particular need or weakness, Selke would try to choose the proper player convenient to their solution. A goalie may be placed with a particular team because that was the club's lone weak spot. Alternatively, a goalie needing to see more rubber to improve would be dropped onto a team with porous defense. Forwards with scoring potential would be placed on teams with gaps in their top six, or if the player had matured offensively, he'd then be challenged by a destination that required concentration on two-way play. Defensemen in the system were often sent to work in pairs or with a very experienced minor league partner. They would be placed strictly on clubs who would employ them on all three units.

The affiliate agreements often included a Canadiens-approved or salaried coach to watch over the players and report back. The coaches themselves were judged on the progress of the players. All the agreements Selke made were for one year, and if the situation proved imperfect it lasted no longer.

By the early 1950s, Selke had found the perfect understudy in Sam Pollock, and he groomed him similarly, challenging him with various tasks mostly to do with the younger players. The tricks of the trade were passed on. Pollock coached, scouted and managed in the system; the teams he was charged with winning several championships. When Selke retired, the transition was seamless. Pollock then ran the Canadiens with no change in managerial philosophy, taking several of the players he helped groom with him.

A Closer Inspection of the Canadiens' Assets During the Radius Rule Years

During the 25 Original Six seasons there were approximately 145 players born in the province of Quebec who played at least one NHL game during that period. Of that group, half (72) played for teams other than the Montreal Canadiens, not a surprising total to someone recalling many of those players.

The Bruins found 17 players of varying talent from Quebec, the better known names being Gilles Marotte, Eddie Johnston, Bernie Parent, and Don Marcotte. The Red Wings came up with Pit Martin, Jim Watson, Denis Dejordy, Bill Dineen, Ron Harris, Marcel Bonin and Marcel Pronovost among the 17 they signed. Chicago and Toronto rarely scouted the province, each finding a half dozen players from Quebec. The Black Hawks came away with Elmer Vasko and Pierre Pilote, while the Leafs had Todd Sloan and Dave Keon. The Rangers were quite active in signing Quebec-born players, and it served them well at times. Among the 26 that New York signed were Gump Worsley, Gilles Villemure, Rod Gilbert, Jean Ratelle, Camille Henry, Marcel Paille, Leon Rochefort and Jean-Guy Gendron. Like the Canadiens, their five rivals also found disappointment and players destined at best for their minor league clubs.

In the 25-year span of the territorial radius rule, the Canadiens employed 188 players, 83 of whom were born in Quebec. Eleven of those 83 got their NHL start with one of the other five teams, and the Canadiens either acquired them by trade (5), the Inter-League Draft (2), purchase (3) or by loan (1).

The composition of the 83 Quebec-born players is as interesting as its number is misleading. What appears at first to be a ridiculously impressive quantity of talent reveals a truer nature when dividing those players into five distinct categories. In order to take a closer look at exactly who the Canadiens signed during the years of the radius rule's use, players acquired by the above-mentioned methods will be listed and tallied.

The Canadiens acquired eight Quebec-born players in seven different trades. They were:

- Frank Eddolls of Lachine, acquired from Toronto on September 10, 1943.
- Roger Leger of L'Annonciation, acquired from the Rangers on January 4, 1944.
- Moe White of Verdun came in a trade with the Buffalo Bisons on January 14, 1946.
- Jackie Leclair of Quebec City came from Buffalo on August 17, 1954.
- Jean-Guy Gendron, born in Montreal, was traded by Boston on November 27, 1960.
- Terry Gray, also of Montreal, was acquired in a trade with Chicago on June 7, 1960.
- Gump Worsley of Montreal and Leon Rochefort from Cap-de-la-Madeleine came in a trade with the Rangers on June 4, 1963.

There were five players acquired via Inter-League drafts and one dispersal draft.

- Ken Mosdell from Montreal arrived via the Americans dispersal draft of September 11, 1943.
- Jimmy Peters, born in Montreal, was taken from Buffalo in the Inter-league draft June 14, 1945.

- Bob Perreault of Trois-Rivières came from Providence in the Inter-league draft on June 11, 1953.
- Phil Goyette of Lachine came in the Inter-league draft from the Montreal Royals on June 5, 1956.
- Marcel Bonin of Montreal was taken from Springfield in the Inter-league draft on June 4, 1957.

Four players were purchased by the Canadiens.

- Murph Chamberlain of Shawville was purchased from Toronto on May 10, 1940.
- Fern Gauthier of Chicoutimi was purchased from the AHL Washington Lions on February 8, 1942.
- Jean-Paul Lamirande of Shawinigan was purchased from Chicago on October 25, 1954.
- Connie Broden of Montreal was purchased from Springfield on October 10, 1957.

The Canadiens were granted the use of 16 players, all but one through minor league loans. The Watson deal was a conditional loan for loan, one-year arrangement.

- Ernie Laforce of Montreal was loaned for one game from the Montreal Royals on March 4, 1943.
- Bobby Lee of Verdun was loaned for one game from the Montreal Royals on December 19, 1942.
- Frank Mailley of Lachine played one game on loan from Washington Lions on December 23, 1942.
- Phil Watson from Montreal was loaned from the Rangers on October 27, 1943, for the full season.
- Rosario Joanette of Valleyfield was loaned for two games by Valleyfield on December 27, 1944.
- Nils Tremblay of Matane came on a one-game loan from Quebec Aces on March 21, 1945.
- Gerry Desaulniers of Shawinigan played eight games on several loans from Montreal Royals, beginning on December 1, 1950.

- Cliff Malone of Quebec City was loaned for three games from Montreal Royals on January 19, 1952.
- Hal Murphy of Montreal was loaned for one game from the Montreal Royals on November 8, 1952.
- Roland Rousseau of Montreal was loaned for two games by the Royals on December 31, 1952.
- André Corriveau of Grand Mère played three games on loan from Valleyfield on January 20, 1954.
- Guy Rousseau of Montreal was loaned for four games from the Quebec Aces on December 16, 1954.
- Jim Bartlett of Verdun was loaned for two games from Chicoutimi on January 4, 1955.
- André Binette of Montreal was loaned for one game by the Montreal Royals on November 11, 1954.
- Claude Evans of Longueuil was loaned for four games by the Royals on November 13, 1954.
- Claude Cyr of Montreal was loaned for one game from Hull-Ottawa on March 19, 1959.

A further group of 16 players signed by the Canadiens had little impact in the grander scheme and played less than 50 games during their career with the team. Most of these players signed their C-Forms years ahead of when they would graduate to the Canadiens. The information listed below is as such: Player; hometown; seasons in which they played for the Canadiens; number of games played; junior affiliate and the year they were assigned to it.

- John Mahaffy of Montreal: (1942-44/9 games); Montreal Royals 1934.
- Tod Campeau of St. Jerome: (1943-49/42 games); Montreal Royals 1942.
- Gilles Dube of Sherbrooke: (1949-50/12 games); Senior Canadiens 1946.
- Claude Robert of Montreal: (1950-51/23 games); Montreal Royals 1948.
- Fred Burchell of Montreal: (1950-54/4 games); Montreal Royals 1947.

- Tom Manastersky of Montreal: (1950-51/6 games); Montreal Royals 1945.
- Ernie Roche of Montreal: (1950-51/4 games); Junior Canadiens 1946.
- Jacques Deslauriers of Montreal: (1955-56/2 games); Cincinnati Mohawks 1949.
- Claude Laforge of Sorel: (1957-58/5 games); Junior Canadiens 1954.
- Claude Pronovost of Shawinigan: (1958-59/2 games); Montreal Royals 1953.
- Reggie Fleming of Montreal: (1959-60/3 games); Senior Canadiens 1953.
- Wayne Connolly of Rouyn: (1960-61/3 games); Peterborough Petes 1956.
- Jean-Guy Morrissette of Causapscal: (1963-64/1 game); Omaha Knights 1963.
- André Boudrias of Montreal: (1963-67/7 games); Hull/Ottawa Canadiens 1960.
- Noel Picard of Montreal: (1964-65/16 games); Omaha Knights 1963.
- Carol Vadnais of Montreal: (1966-68/42 games); Junior Canadiens 1964.

On the 1942-43 and 1943-44 Canadiens, there were nine players who were signed by the organization prior to October 1942 and would thereby not qualify as players scouted and signed under the radius rule. They are listed with their hometowns and season span in a Canadiens uniform.

- Buddy O'Connor of Montreal: 1941-47
- Emile Bouchard of Montreal: 1941-56
- Maurice Richard of Montreal: 1942-60
- Tony Demers of Chambly: 1938-43
- Red Goupille of Trois-Rivières: 1935-43
- Paul Bibeault of Montreal: 1940-46
- Gerry Heffernan of Montreal: 1942-44
- Fern Majeau of Verdun: 1943-45
- Bob Filion of Thetford Mines: 1943-50

Subtracting all of the players who were signed prior to 1942, those acquired by trade, those drafted, those purchased and obtained by loan, and those who played in less than fifty games, there are 25 players remaining. These players would form the francophone core of the Canadiens teams from 1944 to 1967 and beyond. The information listed below is as follows: Birthplace, year signed and years playing for Canadiens, where the player played when signed, and where Canadiens placed him first. Note (*) that 14 of the 25 players' birthplaces are outside Montreal's fifty-mile radius.

- Gerry Plamondon of Sherbrooke: (1943/1945-51), Junior Canadiens/Valleyfield Braves*
- Leo Gravelle of Aylmer: (1945/1946-51), St. Michael's Majors/ Montreal Sr. Royals*
- Jacques Locas of Pointe-Aux-Trembles: (1943/1947-49), Concordia Civics/Montreal Sr. Royals*
- Doug Harvey of Montreal: (1942/1947-61), Montreal Jr. Royals/ Montreal Sr. Royals
- Gerry McNeil of Quebec City: (1943/1947-57), Montreal Jr. Royals/Montreal Sr. Royals*
- Bernie Geoffrion of Montreal: (1951/1950-64), Montreal Concordia/Montreal National
- Jean Beliveau of Trois-Rivières: (1950/1950-71), Victoriaville Tigres/Quebec Aces*
- Dollard St. Laurent of Verdun: (1947/1950-58), Junior Canadiens/Montreal Sr. Royals
- Dickie Moore of Montreal: (1947/1951-63), Montreal Jr. Royals/ Junior Canadiens
- Don Marshall of Montreal: (1949/1951-63), Junior Canadiens/ Cincinnati Mohawks
- Jacques Plante of Shawinigan: (1947/1952-63), Quebec Citadelles/Montreal Sr. Royals*
- Jean-Guy Talbot of Cap-de-la-Madeleine: (1949/1954-67), Trois-Rivieres Reds/Quebec Aces*
- Charlie Hodge of Lachine: (1949/1954-67), Junior Canadiens/ Cincinnati Mohawks

- Henri Richard of Montreal: (1951/1956-75), Montreal National/ Junior Canadiens
- Claude Provost of Montreal: (1951/1955-70), Montreal National/ Junior Canadiens
- Andre Pronovost of Shawinigan: (1953/1956-61), Verdun Canadiens/Junior Canadiens*
- Albert Langlois of Magog: (1952/1957-61), Quebec Citadelles/ Quebec Frontenacs*
- J.C. Tremblay of Bagotville: (1957/1959-72), Hull-Ottawa Jr. Canadiens/H-O Sr. Canadiens*
- Gilles Tremblay of Montmorency: (1956/1960-69), Hull-Ottawa Jr. Canadiens/H-O Sr. Canadiens*
- Bobby Rousseau of Montreal: (1956/1960-70), St. Jean Braves/ Hull-Ottawa Jr. Canadiens
- Jean Gauthier of Montreal: (1955/1960-67), St. Boniface Canadiens/Hull-Ottawa Sr. Canadiens
- Jacques Laperriere of Rouyn: (1958/1962-74), Hull-Ottawa Jr. Canadiens/Brockville Canadiens*
- Yvan Cournoyer of Drummondville: (1961/1963-79), Lachine Maroons/Junior Canadiens*
- Serge Savard of Montreal: (1963/1966-81), Junior Canadiens/ Omaha Knights
- Rogatien Vachon of Palmarolle: (1963/1966-72), Montreal Monarchs/Junior Canadiens*

There were a further eight assets born in Quebec who were signed by the Canadiens during territorial rule, who played in the five seasons beyond the Original Six years. Of the group, Berry, Charron, Grenier, Comeau and Gagnon all played 25 games or less.

- Jacques Lemaire of Lasalle: (1963/1967-79), Lachine Maroons/ Junior Canadiens
- Bob Berry of Montreal: (1963/1968-69), Verdun Maple Leafs/ Peterborough Petes
- Christian Bordeleau of Noranda: (1963/1968-70), Noranda Copper Kings/Junior Canadiens*
- Guy Lapointe of Montreal: (1965/1968-82), Verdun Maple Leafs/Junior Canadiens

- Guy Charron of Verdun: (1966/1969-71), Verdun Maple Leafs/ Junior Canadiens
- Lucien Grenier of Malartic: (1963/1970-71), Notre Dame Monarchs/Junior Canadiens*
- Reynald Comeau of Montreal: (1965/1971-72), West Island Flyers/Verdun Maple Leafs
- Germain Gagnon of Chicoutimi: (1961/1971-72), Lachine Maroons/Hull-Ottawa Canadiens*

There were more players born in the province of Quebec who appeared with the Canadiens from 1967-68 up until 1971-72. None were signed to C-Forms or acquired under territorial rule. Those names would include Alain Caron and Denis DeJordy, who arrived via trades, and Jude Drouin, Phil Myre, Pierre Bouchard, Rejean Houle, Marc Tardif and Guy Lafleur, who were each selected in the NHL Amateur Draft.

In sum, the Canadiens players born in the province of Quebec within a 50-mile radius of Montreal who were signed during the territorial rule and played more than fifty games for the team were Doug Harvey, Bernie Geoffrion, Dollard St. Laurent, Dickie Moore, Donnie Marshall, Charlie Hodge, Henri Richard, Claude Provost, Bobby Rousseau, Jean Gauthier, Serge Savard, Jacques Lemaire and Guy Lapointe.

French and English in Harmony

Had the league not instigated the territorial radius rule in 1942, it is likely that the Canadiens would have continued to C-Form all the francophone players they could find regardless of whether or not they had been given the added window of privilege by the league ruling. They had pounced all over players who had proven to be less than adequate for years. Why would they not act similarly when the real deal presented itself?

The 50-mile radius rule allowed the Canadiens to sign players up until the age of 20 in their designated region. They had previously signed some at younger ages and continued to do so, signing them often as early as age 15. The radius rule altered little in consequence to Canadiens finding legitimate talent. They approached matters the same as they always had. If anything, in the case of certain players slower to develop, the ruling provided for an added few seasons to make proper evaluations.

It wasn't as though the five other NHL clubs were about to spend thousands of dollars scouring the Quebec wastelands where few prospects had ever been found. They would spend their time and money elsewhere, where the results were more proven. Similarly, the Canadiens did not become irrational, spending innumerable amounts of cash to sign every player in the province to C-Forms, contrary to a famous statement made by Bernie Geoffrion some years later. A thousand players signed to hundred-dollar C-Forms would get costly in a hurry. The Canadiens would wait several years after the implementation of the radius rule before investing more heavily.

But the Canadiens did not become perennial contenders strictly on the backs of the Quebec-born players they found in the Original Six era. Those particular players did, as virtual hometown talents, gain the most notoriety, but the contributions of players from outside the province were equally integral to team success. Close to 60 percent of the composition of the club over the course of the Original Six Era was made up of outside, English-speaking players who along with numerous Anglophone Montreal players fit perfectly into the mix. Curiously, the players seemed to come from many of the same regions, establishing further cohesion. Gorman, Selke and Pollock were aligned in their selectiveness, getting the Western stock Irvin adored in addition to players from Blake's neck of the Ontario woods. A quick look at what would be considered the best 20 non-francophone contributors from the era shows incredible consistency. The players with asterisks were acquired in trades.

- Ken Reardon (1940-50) Winnipeg, Manitoba 341/31 games, 1 Stanley Cup
- Elmer Lach (1940-56) Nokomis, Saskatchewan 664/76 games, 3 Stanley Cups
- Toe Blake* (1935-58) Victoria Mines, Ontario 569/572 games, 2 Stanley Cups

- Bill Durnan (1943-50) Toronto, Ontario 383/45 games, 2 Stanley Cups
- Glen Harmon (1942-51) Holland, Manitoba 452/53 games, 2 Stanley Cups
- Floyd Curry (1947-58) Chapleau, Ontario 601/91 games, 4 Stanley Cups
- Tom Johnson (1947-63) Baldur, Manitoba 857/111 games, 6 Stanley Cups
- Billy Reay* (1945-53) Winnipeg, Manitoba 475/63 games, 2 Stanley Cups
- Bert Olmstead* (1950-58) Sceptre, Saskatchewan 508/86 games, 4 Stanley Cups
- Bob Turner (1955-61) Regina, Saskatchewan 339/50 games, 5 Stanley Cups
- Ralph Backstrom (1956-71) Kirkland Lake, Ontario 844/100 games, 6 Stanley Cups
- Bill Hicke (1958-65) Regina, Sasktchewan 318/31 games, 2 Stanley Cups
- Terry Harper (1963-72) Regina, Saskatchewan 554/94 games, 5 Stanley Cups
- Claude Larose (1962-75) Hearst, Ontario 529/82 games, 5 Stanley Cups
- Dave Balon* (1963-67) Wakaw, Saskatchewan 226/35 games, 2 Stanley Cups
- John Ferguson (1963-71) Vancouver, British Columbia 500/85 games, 5 Stanley Cups
- Ted Harris (1963-70) Winnipeg, Manitoba 407/60 games, 4 Stanley Cups
- Jimmy Roberts (1963-77) Toronto, Ontario 611/101 games, 5 Stanley Cups
- Dick Duff* (1964-70) Kirkland Lake, Ontario 305/60 games, 4 Stanley Cups
- Mickey Redmond (1967-71) Kirkland Lake, Ontario 221/16 games, 2 Stanley Cups

Though many of the French-Canadians on the team proved themselves as strong players throughout the period, the Habs were not dominated by the French players in terms of sheer quantity. For many who feel the Canadiens were continuously unfairly privileged to the detriment of the other clubs, there is enough evidence to the contrary.

The truest story of the Canadiens during the 1950s and '60s was not that of a team brought together by a rule favoring them. It was the story of a hockey club, truly Canadian in spirit, wherein the French and English worked hand in hand to achieve a common goal.

Conn Smythe was at least right about one thing: The English and French could indeed work alongside each other on the battlefield.

6

DRYDEN BRUIN', LAFLEUR UNSEALED AND DIONNE ALMOST UNWINGED

Why on God's Earth Would California Have Thrown Cash into the Deal?

Sam Pollock, or Trader Sam as he became known, was considered a genius in his managerial domain and was often recognized for his flair in what turned out to be very one-sided deals. That the Canadiens were able to maintain such a high standard of excellence under his watch might be because Pollock had not only a keen eye for talent and a certain tunnel vision, but he often seemed born under a lucky star.

Those speaking of Pollock's brilliance often make mention of the robbery he committed at the hands of the California Golden Seals in the 1970 draft that enabled the Canadiens to land Guy Lafleur. As legend goes, a series of tricky plot maneuvers engineered by Pollock twelve months prior to the 1971 lottery for Lafleur were done totally by design. On May 22, he dealt prospect Ernie Hicke, the Habs' first pick and the tenth pick overall, to California for a player named Lacombe, a cash sum, and the Seals' first-round pick in 1971, which they used to select Lafleur.

Why on God's Earth would California have thrown cash into the deal?

In the 1970 draft, the Seals did not own a first-round pick, having traded it away. The Canadiens were picking fifth, sixth and tenth. After the Sabres selected Gilbert Perreault with their first overall pick, Pollock used his first two choices on goalie Ray Martyniuk and forward Chuck Lefley, bypassing the highly touted Darryl Sittler and Chris Oddleifson. Oddleifson was no slouch. Playing for the WCHL's Winnipeg Jets, he had scored 95 points in 59 games. Figuring he could swing a deal for him, Seals GM Frank Selke Jr. contacted the man who was once his father's understudy and made an offer. So badly did he desire Oddleifson, Selke added a lump of cash to induce Pollock into the deal. The Habs GM needed little urging, knowing full well the quality of play Oddleifson had to offer.

Where the tale gained an even larger legend was in the following season, when Pollock added a second wrinkle to his acquisition of Lafleur. As this slice goes, it is told that he was concerned about the Seals leapfrogging the Los Angeles Kings at the bottom of the standings. The Boston Bruins owned the Kings' pick and would use it to select Lafleur or Marcel Dionne. Nearing the end of January, he dealt forward Ralph Backstrom to L.A. for a pair of minor league players, and soon the Kings began winning more regularly. When the inevitable happened and the Seals were left in the dust, everyone applauded Trader Sam's shrewdness.

Only once again, it didn't quite happen that way. A quality two-way center, Backstrom had been stuck in the Canadiens' depth chart behind Jean Beliveau and Henri Richard for years. Not only did this hurt his point production, but also it affected his ability to negotiate a higher salary. He had many times asked to be traded to a team in which he would be more appreciated and better paid. Twice Pollock had promised and seemingly reneged. Prior to the beginning of the '70-71 season, Backstrom informed Pollock that he was retiring, which prompted another promise from the manager. Come January, when Pollock had still failed to deliver, the unhappy player quit. It was at this point that Pollock finally decided to act and gave his player the option of destinations. Backstrom conferred with his wife, who loved the sunshine, and relayed to the GM that either California-based club was good with him. Of course Sam couldn't deal Backstrom to the Seals and kill his own draft pick, so Ralph became a King.

Pollock, Selke Jr. and Backstrom have all set the different records straight several times, but despite this, history has chosen to perceive the legend as fact.

Shortly following Pollock's passing in 2007, a third layer to the story emerged, courtesy of Coach Scotty Bowman. It shows that even the greatest minds are not infallible. As Bowman told it, the Detroit Red Wings were very high on rugged Canadiens defenseman Terry Harper. Ned Harkness, who had recently been appointed GM of the Wings, was looking to make a splash. He offered his first-round pick, which turned out to be the second pick overall, for Harper, fleet-footed blue liner J.C. Tremblay and two other roster players Bowman could not recall. Pollock rounded up his hockey men—scouts Ron Caron and Claude Ruel, and Bowman, who had yet to coach a game for the Canadiens—and asked the following question: "What would you think if I told you that there's an opportunity to have again what we had with Beliveau and Geoffrion?"

Pollock was referring to the deadly combination of two young players of perfectly suited chemistry that the Habs debuted starting in 1953. Pollock assuredly had visions of multiple Stanley Cups dancing in his head as he thought of the prospect of nabbing both Lafleur and Marcel Dionne. As he explained the deal to his think tank, they stood silently before him, pondering for long seconds. Finally, one of the scouts opined, "That's an awful lot of experience on defense to give up in one trade!" Pollock then reconsidered.

Hearing of this, Dionne was beside himself. The man who went on to score 731 goals in the NHL had only then learned how close he had come to being a Canadien. "Seriously? I would have scored a thousand goals with that team had they drafted me!"

Another Pollock theft with a twist occurred under considerably less limelight. It came in 1964, and this time it was the Boston Bruins who were unsuspecting victims. The Canadiens manager, who would later earn a reputation for working the phone lines like a zealot come time to make a trade, had not even planned to make a deal. On this day, about all Sam had to do was pick up the phone and say "Yes!"

It was around this same time that a final French-Canadian player provision was granted to the Canadiens for a seven-year period. Though it does not necessarily play into the story, it is best explained in the context of its time.

The NHL Amateur Draft, as it was then known, was a very rudimentary process in its beginnings. Held with little fanfare at the Queen Elizabeth Hotel in Montreal on June 11, 1964, the six NHL clubs would select amateur talent that had not been placed on any type of sponsorship or reserve lists prior to May 1 of that year. This was the second such draft of its kind held by the League and involved only 16- and 17-year-old players born between Aug. 1, 1947, and July 1, 1948. With most of the top-end talent of that age group already considered to have been signed, the Amateur Draft was then regarded as an afterthought by the press, who did not attend. The following day, the *Montreal Gazette* reported that it had taken place but gave no details as to which players had been chosen. In two sentences printed about the Canadiens, the paper erred in reporting how the club proceeded.

"Montreal Canadiens, under draft regulations, had first and second choices for priority rights to any player who is the son of a French-Canadian father. The Montreal club exercised its option fully; it did not last year when the amateur draft was inaugurated."

In fact, the Canadiens did not use the clause on this day, selecting sixth in each of the four rounds of the draft. They would not make use of the wrongly stated clause until 1968, when they chose Michel Plasse and Roger Belisle with the first two selections, doing the same again for Rejean Houle and Marc Tardif in 1969.

By 1963, the NHL had by then understood that it would one day expand the size of its league and do away completely with each club's 50-mile territorial radius rule. To enable both changes, there would be a phasing out of the C-Form method of contracting players concurrent with a phasing in of a more universal draft, which occurred starting in 1969. The League required unanimous approval to pass this amendment, as Pollock was the sole holdout among the six team managers.

Pollock's contention was that the Canadiens had too much invested financially in the feeder system they had built up more than any other club, to simply allow the current format to run its course. His logic was that Montreal would ultimately be sacrificing the most players to the better good of the League once reserve clauses were rolled back, the C-Form phased out and the universal draft implemented. He wanted an additional protective measure for the seven years until that time. Figuring that Pollock and the Canadiens had already picked Quebec clean of French-Canadians, as was their tendency, the other NHL governors figured little was left over for them to pick from.

And they weren't far off in thinking so. In the first six years of the amateur draft's existence, a total of 122 unsigned prospects were selected by the six, and later 12, NHL teams. Of that number, 43 players would make it to the NHL for at least one game. Between 1963 and 1968, the Canadiens chose a total of 18 players, five of whom would make the NHL. They were: Garry Monahan (1963); Pierre Bouchard (1965); Phil Myre and Jude Drouin (1966) and Michel Plasse (1968). All but Monahan were French-Canadian. Of the remaining thirteen selections, Montreal chose French-Canadian players on only three other occasions. In 1964 they selected Claude Chagnon and Michel Jacques, and in '68 they took Belisle. By 1969, the league-wide universal drafting of 20-year-olds had been implemented, and Montreal used Pollock's wrinkle a second and final time to select Houle and Tardif.

Other NHL teams fared pretty well over the six years of this draft, which League president Clarence Campbell stated was devised to "even the playing field." In 1963, Detroit chose center Peter Mahovlich, immediately after the Canadiens had taken a chance on Monahan. That same year, Toronto snapped up all of Walt McKechnie, Jim McKenny and Gerry Meehan and added Mike Pelyk in 1964. The Rangers scored that same year with Tim Ecclestone and Syl Apps Jr. In 1966, the Leafs added Rick Ley. Boston, picking first in each round that year, came up with four future NHLers in Barry Gibbs, Rick Smith, Garnet Bailey and Tom Webster. The Rangers might have fared even better, taking Brad Park, Joey Johnson and Don Luce. In 1967, Toronto grabbed Bob "Battleship" Kelly and the Flyers found Serge Bernier, from Quebec, right under the Canadiens' noses. In 1968, the St. Louis Blues snapped up goalie Gary Edwards and forward Curt Bennett, and the Leafs got defenseman Brad Selwood.

Standing head and shoulders above these names was the goaltender for the Humber Valley Packers of the Metro Toronto Hockey League. Qualifying for the 1964 draft by a mere seven days,

16-year-old Ken Dryden was born on August 8, 1947. He was play-ing right in the heart of Maple Leafs territory at the time, and Toronto had certainly seen him play often enough, as he was a teammate of Conn Smythe's grandson on the Packers. The area was also on the Bruins' radar, as they had a highly touted pros-pect named Bobby Orr, playing in nearby Oshawa. As all teams had failed to get Dryden under contract, he became eligible for the 1964 amateur draft.

Approaching the draft, the Bruins had their sights set on select-ing a defenseman named Guy Allen, a six-foot, 200-pound teen who had played for the Stamford Jr. B club. The Canadiens upset those plans by taking Allen twelfth overall. Wren Blair, the scout for the Bruins, was peeved that Allen had gotten away from him and also knew Dryden better than most at the time. He knew that Dryden's career aspirations involved pursuing the university route toward a legal scholarship. When he informed Bruins GM Lynn Patrick that Dryden's career priorities did not include hockey, the manager phoned Pollock to suggest a deal. Boston would flip their first and third-round picks (Alex Campbell and Dryden) for the Canadiens' second and fourth-round picks (Allen and Paul Reid). Pollock agreed.

Dryden, as it is known, went on to win six Stanley Cups in a little over eight NHL full seasons with Montreal. He is a Hockey Hall of Famer, his jersey having been raised to the Bell Centre rafters among other Canadiens immortals. Allen, Reid and Campbell all found their way into NHL rinks only as paying customers. None of them ever played a single game in the NHL.

Shortly after the 2007 ceremony that saw Dryden's number 29 retired, he spoke with Bertrand Raymond of *Le Journal de Montreal*. Having played three seasons for Cornell University, during which time he had performed countless times in the Boston Garden's confines, the goalie expressed his initial disbelief upon discovering that he had actually been drafted by the Bruins.

"It was a very private draft in those days," Dryden said. "I only found out about it one week later. The funniest part is that my Junior B coach informed me that I had been taken by the Canadiens. It wasn't until 1974 that I found out otherwise." During a passing conversation with Habs statistician Camille Desroches, it was mentioned to him that he had in fact been a Bruins draft pick in 1964. Dryden was perplexed. "I didn't know that I'd been traded for. They kept me in the dark about this for almost ten years." The scouts then explained to him what happened on that fateful day, and how the Bruins desperately wanted Guy Allen. Dryden admits that since the day he found this out, Allen's name has never left his consciousness, simply because this mysterious player, unknown to him, had drastically affected the outcome of his entire life.

Long after Dryden had become a lawyer, a respected author, and the Toronto Maple Leafs president and assistant general manager, he ran for the York Center Riding and was elected to the Canadian Parliament. On the campaign trail a few years later, someone from a crowded scrum asked the former goalie if the name Guy Allen had any significance to him. Dryden bolted upright, "Well, of course, the man changed my life!" Allen, until then a mysterious figure for the goalie, stood before him.

Allen had gone on to play junior hockey with Niagara Falls, and his hockey playing days had ended there. He returned home to Timmins, Ontario, to become a fireman. It was only a few years after Dryden's election that the legend finally met up with the man who altered his career.

Prior to trading Dryden to Montreal, the Bruins had rarely ever neared the Stanley Cup. When they did make the playoffs, they often ran headlong into a Canadiens squad that would upset them as underdogs, or dominate them as favorites. It seemed only logical then that Raymond asked Dryden how he felt his career would have unfolded had he remained Bruins' property.

"I don't even want to think about it," laughed Dryden. He then pointed out that every single detail of his career had played out perfectly. His life has never lacked spice and excitement, and all his hockey dreams were fulfilled simply by landing with the Canadiens organization at the perfect time. Whenever he is asked if there were regrets during his career, he will interrupt the question in mid-sentence.

"Consider that an athlete has no choice in where he begins to play, and that careers for all intents are usually on average, quite short. I had the chance to belong to the Montreal Canadiens, to

Dryden, Ken #29

play in the Forum, and live in Quebec in the nineteen-seventies. Who do you know that would have regrets, had their life unfolded this way? Myself, I never regretted a single minute. Never mind what would have gone down had I gone to Boston instead. I'm just happy things went the way they did."

Dryden, no doubt, could have sat and talked all day with Pollock, Lafleur and Dionne. Serendipity would have made for an interesting topic.

Montreal Canadiens locker room display (Ken Dryden) at the Hockey Hall of Fame, photographed in Toronto, Ontario, Canada on July 24, 2010. *Author: Michael Barera*

7

A DYNASTY UNDONE—WHAT BECAME OF THE 1970S CANADIENS

From You, With Failing Hands, We Fumble the Torch

The Montreal Canadiens' last dynasty officially ended on April 27, 1980, with a 3-2 loss to the Minnesota North Stars. It is no understatement to say that for fans of the Canadiens and hockey in general the loss represented the end of an era.

The Canadiens team of 1979-80 was not an old club based on the individual ages of the players, but they were certainly an aged group in terms of playoff wear and tear. Only three members of that year's edition were 30 or older, and of the 28 players employed on the season whole, 16 were age 25 or younger. What on the surface appeared to be a perfect blend of youth and experience was indeed misleading. After multiple playoff wars, this was a beaten down and often injured group. In the Game 7 loss to Minnesota, injuries to four key players, including a pair of 50-goal scorers, foretold the Canadiens future. Its charges needed to be replenished, but only a keen eye could have noticed what had not yet become apparent; that Montreal would soon be dealing in diminishing assets.

GM Sam Pollock and Coach Scotty Bowman were no longer at the helm of the club, and the previous spring, immediately following the fourth consecutive Cup, goalie Ken Dryden and forwards

Yvan Cournoyer and Jacques Lemaire had all retired. The five subtractions taken together left the club with huge voids. Replacing legendary players is difficult enough in its own right, but hockey men of Pollock and Bowman's stature and expertise simply aren't walking the streets of Montreal.

The 1979-80 Canadiens had finished the regular season with a record of 47-20-13 for 107 points. A drop of 22 points from two seasons prior was enough to set off alarm bells. At the time, there was no such term as a "Stanley Cup hangover" to describe slow starts the season following a Cup win. When the Habs trudged out of the gate with a deceiving 15-9-6 record after 30 games, newly appointed head coach Boomer Geoffrion called it quits. Happening only two weeks into December of 1979, these were the first cracks in the armor showing that all was not right inside the Forum.

An organizational transfer, which began in 1978, is where the Habs fumbled the ball. For some time, Pollock had planned to leave the organization, and he was charged by ownership with choosing his successor. Mired in this passing of the torch was the fact that ownership of the team was also about to change. Brothers Peter and Edward Bronfman had acquired the franchise from the Molson family in 1971 and were preparing to sell the team back to Molson breweries. The Bronfman brothers, as a company, were moving into the realm of larger real estate holdings and would bring Pollock with them. While the legendary manager's genius defined him as a hockey man, the essence of his portfolio spoke for him as a brilliant business mind. The Bronfman family was prepared to pay much more for Sam's instincts and vision than the Molsons were ready to offer.

Times were rapidly changing, and old-school thinking was on the way out. When Molson Brewery completed the transaction, Pollock agreed to stay on for an additional season in a consultant's role, in order to advise his successor on the many facets of inner NHL workings.

Subsequently, Sam chose Irving Grundman and proceeded to groom him as his successor. Grundman was not a popular choice by any stretch. He had zero hockey acumen in the eyes of most observers. As a businessman, he was best known for his Laurentian Lanes chain of bowling alleys in Quebec, from which he had gained his wealth. During a season of transition, both Pollock and Grundman had sat down with Bowman to discuss his future with the Canadiens, and the possibility of his eventual ascendance to the position of GM of the club himself. Grundman told the coach that he would only serve as the team's GM for about five or six years and that Bowman would indeed succeed him over time. The pair had a year to work together and find a semblance of harmony before the coach's contract ran out. In that time, Bowman branded him as a "glorified bowling alley manager." The term stuck to Grundman like a birthmark.

Years later, after his departure from the Canadiens, Bowman discussed his differences with Grundman, though he offered little in terms of details as to their butting of heads.

"There was no room for Irving Grundman and me on the same team," Bowman told the *Montreal Gazette*. "It was a power struggle that I could have won over the years if we'd started from the same point, but he had the lead. It was better for them and for me that I go. It had reached the point where I couldn't tolerate any further deterioration of my personal situation. It was a question of hockey philosophy. I was convinced I had the competence to be general manager, and I couldn't tolerate the way Grundman directed the club. He said he had a lot of respect for me as coach; I had some for him as a businessman, but I have no respect for him as a hockey man and I couldn't continue in this way."

Following the expiration of his contract with the Canadiens in the summer of 1979, Bowman was offered a lucrative deal to take over the Buffalo Sabres, as both coach and manager of the club. His decision to leave was announced on July 11, and for many, that date would be the official end of the Canadiens dynasty.

No Template in Dynasty Management, No Legendary Trade Returns

Given decades of hindsight, the Bowman split with the Canadiens is noteworthy in the altering of their historical course. Speculation raises open-ended questions, but if Bowman had been given the GM reins and proceeded to trade players prior to when Pollock or Grundman chose to make moves, would the Canadiens have been better off in the long-term?

Though there can be no definitive answer to such a question, it is interesting to note the return that the Canadiens did gain by trading certain players from the core of the '70s dynasty when they did. Whether the club waited too long in trading them is best determined by the assets their trades returned. The Canadiens' predicament was a most unique circumstance: there has never been a template for dynasty management. When Pollock was admittedly challenged by changing times, perhaps Bowman's vision might have served the Canadiens best. If anything, Grundman's reign tells that in certain cases the Canadiens might have hung on to players well past their best before dates.

As an exercise into the continuity of asset management, a look at what became of the Canadiens dynasty provides an interesting view as to what could have possibly been managed differently. It involves a discussion of 30 mostly key players who participated in the five Stanley Cups won between 1973 and 1979.

The group of 30 players divides itself into two groups of 15. The first group consists of players from whom the Canadiens received no dividend whatsoever as they all left the organization under varying scenarios or simply retired. While many were simply destined or preordained to retire as career-long Canadiens, others could have been moved before reaching that point and provided the club with some form of tangible assets moving forward.

The second group of 15 comprises players for whom the Canadiens received compensation, and in many cases earned a solid return on, even in trickle-down transactions. Taken all together, the departures and returns demonstrate what happened to the dynasty. In the long range, this situation led to diminishing returns and prevented the Canadiens from maintaining previous heights. Although they have managed two more Stanley Cups since then, that depth has never been replaced.

The players in the first group include 11 Hall of Famers. They left the Canadiens with no return value to the team. They are:

- Marc Tardif: At age 24, jumped to the WHA's Los Angeles Sharks for the 1973-74 season.
- Jacques Laperriere: Retired at age 33 in 1974, from career-ending knee injury.

120

- Frank Mahovlich: At age 36, jumped to the WHA's Toronto Toros for the 1974-75 season.
- Henri Richard: Retired at age 39, following the 1974-75 season.
- Yvan Cournoyer: Retired at age 36 in 1979, following career-ending back injury.
- Ken Dryden: Retired at age 31, following the 1978-79 season.
- Jacques Lemaire: Retired at age 33, following the 1978-79 season.
- Serge Savard: Retired at age 36, following the 1980-81 season.
- Pierre Mondou: Retired at age 34 in 1985, following career-ending eye injury.
- Rejean Houle: Retired at age 34, following the 1982-83 season.
- Guy Lafleur: Retired at age 34, during the 1984-85 season.
- Steve Shutt: Retired at age 33, following the 1984-85 season.
- Mario Tremblay: Retired at age 30 in 1986, following career-ending shoulder injury.
- Bob Gainey: Retired at age 36, following the 1988-89 season.
- Larry Robinson: At age 38, signed as a free agent with L.A. Kings for the 1989-90 season.

Following the 1973 Stanley Cup, both Tardif and Houle jumped to the WHA, lured by higher salaries. Pollock could have done little about that, as he was unwilling to engage in a salary war with rival league teams that would have upset the Canadiens' salary structure. To that end, however, he did accommodate Lafleur with a ten-year pact the following summer, as well as negotiated a new deal for holdout Ken Dryden, but doing this for less than elite players would have raised unprecedented hell in a harmonious locker room. Perhaps Pollock investigated other options, such as trading the rights to Houle and Tardif together to Buffalo, for a potential reunion with the pair's junior linemate Gil Perreault.

Laperriere retired in 1974 at age 32, following a career-ending knee injury suffered during a game against Boston. Little could have been done to avoid such circumstance. Frank Mahovlich was offered a contract by Pollock in the summer of 1974 but rejected it to accept a higher offer from the WHA's Toronto franchise. The Big M had three or four good seasons of hockey left in him, but the Canadiens chose to hold onto his rights until 1979, when he made a comeback attempt with Detroit. After being slowed by age and injuries during 1974-75, Henri Richard retired. There was never any question of trading the icon, and rightly so.

Testament to the Canadiens' depth, the loss of the five players mentioned above did little to slow the development of the group into a powerhouse. Houle rejoined the club as a free agent in 1976 and along with seven of the ten remaining players listed was a member of the team that lost to Minnesota in April of 1980.

Three players packed it in almost all at once following the '78-79 campaign. Captain Yvan Cournoyer, at age 35, retired due to a bad back. A superstar in his own right, it is doubtful that the Canadiens would have traded the Roadrunner, a player extremely loyal to the organization. Dryden left the game five years after his holdout season, retiring to a beckoning law career. It might have been an option to trade Dryden to his native Toronto where he could practice law and play, but in some minds that would have been no option at all. All through the goalie's final season, he had kept quiet about his plans.

Evidently, so did shifty two-way center Jacques Lemaire. An unsung player at age 33, Lemaire had just completed the best postseason of his career, and with 23 points in 16 playoff games, he would have made an ideal Conn Smythe recipient. Instead, the pivot walked away from the game with lots of hockey left in his tank, to the general surprise of almost everyone, having made his decision to explore overseas coaching avenues.

As is often the case with players having too much mileage on their war-torn bodies, injuries began taking their toll. With four seasons of long playoff runs, several Canadiens players during that span actually played the equivalent of an additional full schedule of games, which were of the most rigorous nature. By the time the Habs lost to the North Stars, the team had played 68 playoff games in five years. Numerous Canadiens were slowing by age 30, their careers in decline. While it was apparent that several ailing players had retained a measure of value, the Canadiens were slow to retool their roster.

Serge Savard was the next player calling it a day in 1981. Early in his career he had suffered two serious leg injuries, and Father Time had caught up to him at age 35. No one would have assumed that he had much value as an asset by that time, but lo and behold, when he was left unprotected in that summer's waiver draft, old pal John Ferguson claimed him for the Winnipeg Jets. It took several weeks of convincing, but Savard made it to Winnipeg in time to play in 123 games over two seasons. The 33-year-old Houle, who had always been a popular teammate and a decent all-around player, retired following an injury-plagued 1982-83 campaign.

Shutt was one season removed from a 35-goal campaign when he became seldom used in Coach Jacques Lemaire's defensive system. He made no waves in approaching Savard, who was by then the club's GM. His former teammate accommodated his wish by trading him to Los Angeles for future considerations. He was 32 at the time, and no attempt seemed to have been made to leverage any value from other potential suitors. The deal to trade Shutt was dependent upon him getting a contract from the Kings for the '85-86 season. He put up 41 points in 59 games with L.A., holding up his end of the bargain. When the Kings offer came in at less than what Shutt would have made as a payoff under the ten-year Canadiens tenure policy, he was traded back to Montreal to retire as a Hab.

A little over a week had passed since the Shutt trade when Guy Lafleur, one of the greatest players to ever play the game, quit in disillusionment. GM Savard, who later admitted that a trade offer from the Buffalo Sabres had been sitting on the table, refused to trade the Flower. An asset such as Perreault would have come in handy as Canadiens players kept dropping like flies.

Pierre Mondou was playing perhaps the best hockey of his career at age 29 when he suffered a career-ending eye injury in a game against Hartford in March of 1985. A similar fate befell Mario Tremblay almost one calendar year later, when he tore up his shoulder in a loss to Quebec. The 12-year veteran was out of the game at age 30.

Bob Gainey played out his full career in a Canadiens uniform and retired following the 1988-89 season. As captain, he was a player Montreal would probably not have traded. Defenseman Robinson, another player unlikely to be dealt, ended his tenure at the same time as Gainey—or so it seemed. Robinson's time with the Canadiens ended in controversy. He wanted a two-year deal from Montreal and approached Savard, who was only willing to offer one year. When Robinson balked, the GM pointed out that he would essentially still get two years, as per the team's policy of awarding ten-year veterans an additional season's salary upon retiring from the team, equal to the salary of the final contract year.

While Robinson pondered his future, Savard then tendered him a low-ball offer. After the two exchanged words, Savard then withdrew the offer, making Robinson a free agent. He would go on to sign with the Kings and play three seasons there.

During the tenures of Grundman and Savard, Montreal missed out on opportunities to trade a few stalwarts for future gain, seeming to place a measure of loyalty ahead of the prospect of maximizing assets. In several cases, events conspired against them, and they may well have traded certain players had they not retired without warning or suffered career-ending injuries when they did.

Grundman Reconstructs a New Core

The second group of 15 players includes two Hall of Famers, a trio of Canadiens record holders to this day, a 50-goal scorer, and close to a dozen role players integral to any winning club. Individually, these players are not as iconic as most of the first group, but their contributions to the Canadiens were of great importance. Perhaps the truest measure of their worth is best appreciated by the trade returns they brought to the team. Without a doubt, it was much easier for the Canadiens to move these players as opposed to some of the others, but when considering what the club achieved by dealing away what many view as secondary assets, it can only be speculated what gains could have been made had management been less reluctant to part with players from the first group.

The second group consists of 15 players dealt away or lost in 13 separate transactions by three different general managers. In these transactions, the Canadiens packaged three additional players and as many draft picks. The players are:

- Jimmy Roberts: Traded at age 37 on August 18, 1977, to St. Louis for their third-round choice (Guy Carbonneau) in 1979 Amateur Draft.
- Peter Mahovlich: Traded at age 31 on November 29, 1977, to Pittsburgh with Peter Lee for Pierre Larouche and Peter Marsh.

- Murray Wilson: Traded at age 26 on October 5, 1978, to Los Angeles by Montreal with Montreal's first-round choice (Jay Wells) in 1979 Entry Draft for Los Angeles' first-round choice (Gilbert Delorme) in 1981 Entry Draft.
- Pierre Bouchard: Waivered at age 30 on October 9, 1978, and claimed by Washington in a bungled potential trade scenario by Irving Grundman.
- Bill Nyrop: Traded at age 27 on August 8, 1979, to Minnesota for their second-round choice (Gaston Gingras) in 1979 Entry Draft.
- Rick Chartraw: Traded at age 26 on February 17, 1981, to Los Angeles for their second-round choice (Claude Lemieux) in 1983 Entry Draft.
- Michel Larocque: Traded at age 28 on March 10, 1981, to Toronto for Robert Picard.
- Yvon Lambert: Claimed at age 30 on October 5, 1981, by Buffalo in Waiver Draft.
- Pierre Larouche: Traded at age 26 on December 21, 1981, with Montreal's first- and third-round choices (Sylvain Cote, Bruce Racine) in 1984 Entry Draft to Hartford for their first- and second-round choices (Petr Svoboda, Brian Benning) in 1984 Entry Draft and third-round choice (Rocky Dundas) in 1985 Entry Draft.
- Guy Lapointe: Traded at age 33 to St. Louis for their second-round choice (Sergio Momesso) in 1983 Entry Draft, March 9, 1982.
- Brian Engblom, Doug Jarvis, Rod Langway and Craig Laughlin: Traded on September 9, 1982, to Washington for Rick Green and Ryan Walter. Respective ages of all six players: 27, 27, 25, 25, 26 and 24.
- Doug Risebrough: Traded at age 28 on September 11, 1982, with the second-round choice (Frantisec Musil) to Calgary for Washington's second-round choice (previously acquired/Todd Francis) in 1983 Entry Draft and Calgary's third-round choice (Graeme Bonar) in 1984 Entry Draft.
- Mark Napier: Traded at age 26 on October 28, 1983, with Keith Acton and Toronto's third-round choice (previously acquired/ Ken Hodge Jr.) in 1984 Entry Draft for Bobby Smith October 28, 1983.

The 13 deals above resulted in the return of five players of immediate use to the roster, plus one throw-in and ten draft picks, six of whom became roster players. In total, the Canadiens moved 21 assets to gain 16.

Four of the trades were considered major deals, and in two of them, Montreal gave up twice as many players as they received. The listing of these trades are in chronological order, with the first two coming at the end of Pollock's tenure and the last being one of GM Serge Savard's first moves. The remaining dozen were under Grundman's five-year reign. Two anomalies listed are the waiver losses of Bouchard and Lambert. In the first instance, Grundman had pre-arranged a deal with Washington that would see the player reacquired by the Canadiens the day after the claim, but the GM was unaware that the league had closed that loophole. Lambert was coming off a 54-point season with Montreal in '80-81 when he was mysteriously not placed on the team's protected list.

There are some interesting notes to many of these moves. The Carbonneau pick (44th in 1979) coming from the Roberts trade was a fruitful return that could have gone even better. Four picks later, the Oilers chose late-bloomer Mark Messier.

The '79 draft was one of the richest in league history. The Kings used their 16th pick acquired from Montreal to select Jay Wells. Had the Canadiens retained the selection, they could have used it on sniper Michel Goulet. The 1981 draft was all about the Dale Hawerchuk sweepstakes, and the Canadiens added the Kings pick to the two other first-round picks they had. They chose Mark Hunter with their seventh pick, passing over the likes of Grant Fuhr, James Patrick and Al McInnis. With the 18th pick acquired from the Kings, they chose defenseman Gilbert Delorme.

In October of 1978, Grundman committed the Bouchard snafu but made amends one year later, trading the rights to retired defenseman Bill Nyrop to Minnesota for their 1979 second-round choice. He used the pick on Gaston Gingras. Grundman made out very well with the Chartraw dealt that resulted in Claude Lemieux. Likewise, the dealing of Michel Larocque to Toronto for defenseman Robert Picard on March 10, 1981, initially held some potential. Unfortunately for Picard, that potential materialized when the Canadiens dealt him to Winnipeg.

In a deal completed on December 21, 1981, Grundman appeared to pursue 16-year-old Laval Voisins star Mario Lemieux, who was in the early stages of rewriting junior hockey league record books. Grundman seemed to understand the likeliness that Lemieux would be selected first overall in the 1984 draft. His actions suggested that he projected that Hartford would potentially be one of the weaker clubs come time for the draft. With Lemieux in mind, the Canadiens traded former 50-goal man Pierre Larouche, along with two draft picks, to the Whalers for their first- and second- round picks as well as a 1985 pick. There was no suspense in the end, as Hartford finished 17th out of 21 teams, 28 points ahead of Pittsburgh, who drafted Lemieux in 1984. Grundman had been relieved of his duties by then, replaced by Savard. Selecting fifth overall, Montreal chose Czech defenseman Petr Svoboda.

On September 9, 1982, Grundman shocked all observers when he sent defensemen Rod Langway, Brian Engblom and forwards Doug Jarvis and Craig Laughlin to Washington for Ryan Walter and Rick Green. Triggering the trade and positioning the Habs GM in a tough spot was the American Langway's displeasure at having to pay Quebec taxes. At the onset, just about every hockey analyst felt it was a one-sided deal for the Capitals. That notion became further cemented when Langway went on to win two Norris trophies upon his arrival.

Hindsight reveals some interesting facts when all is said and done. The oft-injured pair of Green and Walter combined to play in 1,200 regular season and playoff games with Montreal. They were with the Canadiens for seven and nine seasons respectively. In that time, Montreal won one Stanley Cup, lost in the '89 final to Calgary and played into the third round on two other occasions. The four players acquired by Washington participated in 1,646 games. Engblom turned out to be a marginal defenseman and was traded by the Capitals one season later. Jarvis lasted a little over three years and Laughlin lasted five. Langway became an icon in Washington, playing eleven seasons. The Norris accolades were an anomaly for a stay-at-home defenseman, but it is curious to note while playing alongside the likes of Savard and Robinson in Montreal that Langway was a plus-66 in his final Canadiens campaign. In his first in Washington, he was an even plus/minus zero. In his time with the Capitals, the club never made it past the second round.

Grundman's final trade of a 1970s asset came in September of 1982, when Doug Risebrough was sent to Calgary for a pair of draft choices in '83 and '84. Montreal used the '84 pick on a six-foot-three, 210-pound right winger named Graeme Bonar, who looked to have the profile of a potential 50-goal scorer. In his final two seasons as a junior, Bonar kept close to a goal per game pace. He was considered among a bumper crop of quality Canadiens prospects until a series of injuries limited him to 29 games in two pro seasons with the baby Habs in Sherbrooke. Sadly, Bonar never regained his touch.

In the summer of 1983, former defenseman Savard then took over as manager, completing his first major trade only weeks into the season. With first overall pick Doug Wickenheiser continuing to disappoint, Savard judged that the team needed to get bigger down the middle. With that in mind, he dealt two-time 40-goal scorer Mark Napier, along with the team's leading point man of two season's back, Keith Acton, to Minnesota for star Bobby Smith. Napier was one of the last links to the Canadiens' Cup win in 1979. Though initially some people believed that Savard had overpaid for Smith, those sentiments quickly vanished when it became apparent that the Habs emerged with a high-caliber player. Wickenheiser, an unfortunate stain on the Grundman resume, was passed on to St. Louis by Savard two months later.

Of the 16 total assets acquired by the trio of managers from the dynasty's trickle-down, 11 went on to play for Montreal. They were comprised of eight players who were members of the 1986 Cup team (Carbonneau, Gingras, Claude Lemieux, Momesso, Svoboda, Green, Walter and Smith) and three who were not (Larouche, Delorme and Picard). That championship club had three holdovers from the dynasty years— Robinson, Gainey and Tremblay.

In a roundabout way, out of all of Grundman's acquisitions, it would be defenseman Picard who would be turned over for perhaps the best trickle down asset of them all. Brought to Montreal at the 1981 trade deadline, Picard's time with the Canadiens got off to a rocky start, his play sloppy and inconsistent. Furthermore, in an incident well documented in Canadiens' lore, Picard happened to be out on the town with Guy Lafleur on the fateful evening that the

Habs star was almost killed in a car accident. Once the unfortunate details surrounding events became known, they reflected poorly on Picard, who had only been acquired two weeks prior.

Grundman could have dealt Picard as soon as the '81 playoffs had ended, but he chose otherwise. The defenseman's play improved, albeit slightly, over the next two seasons. Whereas Picard's worth as an asset might have been weakened following the incident with Lafleur, it later stabilized and gained value. Not long after Serge Savard took over the reins from Grundman, he dealt the lanky defenseman to old pal John Ferguson in Winnipeg, and Picard returned a third-round pick in the 1984 draft.

By drafting Patrick Roy with the acquired third selection, Savard turned the Picard asset into the home run Grundman missed hitting with Mario Lemieux.

Roy to the Rescue

Over the course of the 1983-84 season the Canadiens' scouts were keeping a watchful eye on a sharpshooter named Stephane Richer, one of the few bright lights on a terrible Granby Bisons team in the Quebec junior league. Richer was about all the offense the Bisons had going for them; the club regularly surrendering in the neighborhood of fifty shots nightly.

In one particular game, an odd incident occurred that made them greatly aware of the Granby goaltender being dented with vulcanized rubber. Granby's opponents somehow found themselves on a 3 on 0 breakaway. The helpless goalie, however, stood tall. After kicking out the first shot, he swiftly gloved the rebound destined for the top corner. With no teammates yet in sight, and losing by a bunch, the netminder made a "bring it on" gesture with his trapper and quickly passed the puck to the third opponent trailing on the play. He then proceeded to stone him just as he had the other two.

The goalie's name was Patrick Roy, and Savard used the pick acquired from Winnipeg to select him 50 positions after the Penguins took Lemieux. Little did anyone assume then how Roy would go on to alter the course of Canadiens history.

The rookie Roy, along with Richer, Claude Lemieux and a cast of other first-year players, would band together with the veterans from the previous era to deliver the franchise's 23rd Stanley Cup. It was a win for the ages, with the goalie seemingly coming out of nowhere to deliver a title snuck in the midst of an Oilers dynasty.

The Canadiens steadily improved their regular season standing over the next three seasons, peaking with 115 points and a rematch with Calgary in the '89 final. GM Savard continued to make deals that were to keep the club from going stale, but soon he and his successors in management would be dealing in diminishing assets.

The '86 championship featured several players that trickled down as assets from the '70s dynasty—Gingras, Carbonneau, Momesso, Walter, Green, Smith, Petr Svoboda, Lemieux and Roy. Three seasons later, Gingras and Momesso had departed, and by 1993 only Carbonneau and Roy remained. The returns were becoming continuously slimmer in quality, but from the eventual trading down of these nine assets, the Canadiens ended up benefitting from the use of nearly another thirty players between 1986 and 2008.

Gingras was traded twice. In 1982, he was sent to Toronto for a pick that became Benoit Brunet. He was moved again in '87 to St. Louis for depth defenseman Larry Trader and a pick that became Pierre Sevigny. Brunet hung around until 2001, when he was dealt along with Martin Rucinski to Dallas for Shaun Van Allen and Donald Audette. Neither of Trader, Sevigny, Van Allen or Audette provided for any future assets.

Momesso was also St. Louis-bound come 1988. Dealt along with minor league goalie Vincent Riendeau, the Canadiens received Jocelyn Lemieux, goalie Darrell May and a 1989 draft pick that resulted in the acquisition of Patrice Brisebois. Lemieux, the brother of Claude, was dealt to Chicago for a draft choice that became Charles Poulin. Brisebois was a key contributor until 2004, and was later re-signed for a second stint. The Canadiens did well with Brisebois, but neither May nor Poulin ever played a game in Montreal's system.

Walter and Green were pretty much worn down by the end of the '80s. Walter signed as a free agent with Vancouver in 1991. Green retired following the 1989 season but made a comeback one year later when his rights were traded to Detroit for a draft choice that resulted in the acquisition of Brad Layzell. Similarly, Bobby Smith was traded back to Minnesota in 1990 for someone named Louis

Bernard. Smith gave the North Stars two 46-point seasons, but Montreal received a shameful return for a 30-year-old former first overall pick.

Up until this time in their history, the Canadiens had rarely traded a player that went on to win a Stanley Cup with another team, never mind win the Conn Smythe Trophy. In 1990, Savard and Coach Pat Burns couldn't get the competitive but irritable Claude Lemieux out of town quickly enough. His grating act wearing thin on everyone's nerves, Lemieux was sent to New Jersey for falling star Sylvain Turgeon, who scored a measly 14 goals in two seasons with the Canadiens. Lemieux went on to play close to a thousand games with several other clubs, winning three Cups. Turgeon was left unprotected in the 1992 expansion draft and was mercifully lost to Ottawa.

Late in the '92 campaign, Montreal sent Svoboda to Buffalo for defenseman Kevin Haller. Along with Brisebois, Haller was among the few assets acquired from the long dynasty player thread to figure in the 1993 Cup championship. He would depart not long afterwards to Philadelphia for defenseman Yves Racine, who had counted for 52 points with the Flyers in '93-94. Unfortunately for Racine, his game was left behind in Philly. He moved to San Jose via the waiver wire two seasons later.

In a somewhat acrimonious parting, Carbonneau was dispatched to the Blues in 1994, after jokingly throwing up his middle finger to a journalist following the Habs playoff elimination. The paltry return on Carbonneau was center Jim Montgomery, who in 67 games the previous season found time in a five-week span to center Brett Hull and add 20 points to his stats. The mirage of Montgomery was waived to the Flyers soon after, while Carbonneau went on to play five seasons with Dallas, adding a third Cup to his resume. It was regarded as one of the worst deals Savard had ever made. Unfortunately for him, he wouldn't get to make many more.

In 13 seasons, Serge Savard had put in some stellar work guiding the Canadiens. In the mid-'80s, his management style combined with his vision had straightened out a team that had lost its direction. Though he had made a handful of deals that showed little patience, he'd also made strong ones that perfectly addressed club needs.

Savard drafted extremely well at times, particularly when it came to finding several quality French-Canadians in the team's backyard.

Meager Trickle Downs and Mediocrity: The Crumbs of the Roy Deal

After the 1993 Stanley Cup, expectations in the short term were set at unachievable heights. Within a year, the team had begun to stumble, and Savard moved to right the ship with some major deals. Breaking up part of the team's core, he had his pocket picked on two occasions, and it sent the team spiraling from the playoff picture a mere 24 months after they had won it all.

This was unacceptable in Montreal, and early in the 1995-96 campaign, Savard and Coach Jacques Demers paid the price. Their dual firing set off dominoes of panic, and the next to fall was iconic puck stopper Patrick Roy, the last great link to the group of assets trickling down from the '70s dynasty.

For Canadiens supporters, the trading of Roy remains a sore spot, inasmuch for its controversy at the time as for how it invariably crippled the franchise. In the estimations of some, Roy could be a polarizing figure while tending goal in Montreal and had begun taking up too much space in the context of the team. Savard had been aware of this and had looked into Roy's value on the trade market, just in case things were to sour further. It was while he was working such scenarios that he had the rug pulled from under him.

The matter of Roy then fell into the inexperienced hands of neophyte Rejean Houle. Following the December 2, 1995, blowup between Coach Mario Tremblay and Roy at the Canadiens bench, Houle wasted little time in allowing the situation to fester. Seventy-two hours later, Roy and Captain Mike Keane were traded to the Colorado Avalanche for goalie Jocelyn Thibault and forwards Martin Rucinsky and Andrei Kovalenko. The trade shook the hockey world and rumbled the foundations of the Canadiens faithful.

Thibault was the key to the deal, and at 20 years of age he had the most upside value moving forward. His destiny, however, would not involve filling Roy's shoes in Montreal, and in three years' time he was traded to Chicago. Rucinsky was the immediate revelation of the trade, posting point-per-game numbers in his first season with the Canadiens. Though he could tantalize with his offensive game, he never did match that initial pace, and would last in Montreal for a little over six seasons. Kovalenko disappointed in demeanor and production from the start and was dispatched to Edmonton nine months later for the rugged Scott Thornton.

The trading of Roy to Colorado would allow for more assets to come the Canadiens' way than any other transaction in team history, but due to the deal being so badly conceived from the onset, the trade could be seen as a depressing case study in diminishing assets. When all was said and done, Thibault, Rucinsky and Kovalenko helped provide a trickle down of 13 more player assets, minimal as they sometimes were.

Thornton lasted close to four seasons with the Canadiens and was traded to Dallas for Juha Lind, who managed all of three goals in 47 games with Montreal before running out of NHL alternatives and heading home to Finland. Rucinsky tallied 297 points in 432 games in his Canadiens career. In 2001, he was shipped along with Benoit Brunet to Dallas for Donald Audette and Shaun Van Allen. Audette counted 21 goals in 138 games with Montreal before he was sent packing, released by the midway through the 2003-04 season. Center Van Allen, a defensive specialist, played 54 games with Montreal, and did the job mandated to him. He re-signed with Ottawa the following summer.

Less than three years following the trade, Thibault became the centerpiece of a seven-player deal with the Blackhawks. No longer able to withstand the Montreal pressure, he approached Houle and told him that he wanted out. He was traded along with defenseman Dave Manson and disappointing first-round pick Brad Brown for goalie Jeff Hackett, sturdy rearguard Eric Weinrich, tough guy Alain Nasreddine and a fourth-round pick. Hackett, Weinrich and Nasreddine brought forth such nonentities as Patrick Traverse, Christian Laflamme, Chris Dyment, Mathieu Descoteaux and Niklas Sundstrom in ensuing trades; the latter having the distinction of being the final asset linked to the 1970s dynasty.

Going back to the two separate groups of 15 players from the 1970s championships, those 30 players including 13 Hall of Famers owned by the Canadiens trickled down to just under fifty total assets by the time of the NHL lockout in 2005. Of the lot, Roy became the lone player to enter the Hockey Hall and he and Carbonneau were the only two players participating in both the '86 and '93 Cups. Among the trickle downs, a further seven players acquired were members of the former win and three others were with the latter champions.

Taken in the context of present hockey dealings, the trickle down numbers can appear misleadingly substantial. It appears that on average, the Canadiens were able to translate almost each single asset from the second group of fifteen players into another three bodies as time passed. As a surface assessment, that also appears interestingly fair as far as returns go. But an encompassing view of the near fifty players shows that for the most part, it consisted mainly of also-rans, bit pieces and journeymen.

Beyond the late 1980s, the Canadiens never so much as acquired a third-round pick for these trickle downs, and that is assuredly the simplest and most direct manner to judge their worth. The truth is, the Canadiens received no more than eight impact players from the 13 assets they were able to trade. To that end, Rick Chartraw, Brian Engblom, Doug Jarvis, Rod Langway, Guy Lapointe, Michel Larocque, Pierre Larouche, Peter Mahovlich, Mark Napier, Bill Nyrop, Doug Risebrough, Jimmy Roberts and Murray Wilson were turned over in one way or another for Guy Carbonneau, Pierre Larouche, Claude Lemieux, Rick Green, Ryan Walter, Bobby Smith, Patrick Roy and Jocelyn Thibault.

8

JACQUES DEMERS BEWITCHED BY LEAFS FAN

"Serge! Boys, Come and Get a Look at This!"
The author had a front-row seat for this funny and totally strange anecdote involving Habs coaches Jacques Demers and Mario Tremblay. It certainly was something to witness with your own eyes. The story unfolds in Cornwall, Ontario, on September 17, 1995, during the first-ever game in Colorado Avalanche history. As things go in this twisted tale, the game was an exhibition contest, and the front-row seat was actually in the last row!

The game in question took place in the small city of 50,000 due to several ties the Avalanche had to Cornwall. It was the home of their Aces farm club, but also where Coach Marc Crawford had played junior hockey and later coached the Cornwall Royals. He had also met and married his lovely wife Helene there. An Avalanche scout, former Blackhawks coach Orval Tessier also called Cornwall home. Two years prior, when Crawford was coaching the St. John's Maple Leafs in the AHL, an arena worker's strike had forced the team to play about twenty of its home games on the road. One of those games, against the Canadiens' farm club from Fredericton, drew a sellout crowd.

It is perhaps only fitting, in light of ominous events that transpired later in the evening, that the participants should have ties to Quebec and Toronto!

The excitement for this game was ample on many fronts. Though the Avalanche was the designated home team, the building was filled with Canadiens fans. Colorado's jersey had yet to be unveiled, and there was some excitement to that end, as hockey fans had so far only seen the logo. The Avalanche roster also included former Royal Owen Nolan, who had been drafted first overall by Quebec a few years earlier. Nolan, the first Colorado player to hit the ice, was greeted with loud cheers to begin the evening. Soon, the excitement dropped several notches. When the two teams began to skate in the warm up, there was no sign of Patrick Roy, Vincent Damphousse, Joe Sakic or Peter Forsberg. It would be a typical training camp game after all. Rookies and other hopefuls made up a sizeable chunk of both rosters.

As the teams lined up for the opening faceoff, a fan noted the absence of Jacques Demers behind the Canadiens bench. Initially believing that Demers might have been fired, he then rationed that if that had indeed happened, he certainly would have heard of it. Manning the bench for this game was Charles Thiffault, Demers's assistant coach. That fact might explain why the Canadiens came out so flat. That or the fact that Patrick Labrecque, in goal for Montreal, was no Patrick Roy!

As the first period came to a close with Colorado leading by two, a noticeable scrum had gathered near the top row of Section Q, on the north side of the arena. A stream of curious fans, pens and programs in hand, continued making their way up thirteen rows of stairs to the press area generally taken up by personnel for the local radio broadcasts. Someone had mentioned spotting Serge Savard earlier, as he was seen walking into the Civic Complex in step with Avalanche GM Pierre Lacroix. When fans in the immediate area turned to see what all the fuss was about, they were surprised to find that Savard had slipped discreetly into the box area in mid-game, joined by Demers and various journalists and television personalities including Mario Tremblay. Autograph hounds and fans clasping Roy hockey cards now had something to seek, and the line of well-wishers lasted the duration of the intermission.

Seated just above the patrons in the top row, Demers greeted each fan cordially. Savard backed off, and leaning against the wall he struck up conversations with Tremblay and journalist Bertrand Raymond. The GM seemed amused at the throes of fans pushing up against the cement barrier to greet the coach. Though the second period was about to begin, there remained a good dozen fans milling about, waiting to meet and chat with Demers. As the numbers dwindled and the period got under way, Savard came forth to shake one fan's hand and graciously sign his 1972 Team Canada card.

One fan, patiently waiting for everyone to finish up, had been sitting on the cement step for over ten minutes, chatting with his friend. He was carrying a plastic bag that had a rectangular box inside. As the last two kids bounced down the steps, he sprung up and made his way to Demers. The author overheard pieces of the discussion, which went something like this:

"Bonjour, Jacques! Can I see your Stanley Cup ring?"

"Salut, mon ami! Certainly, you can," came the genteel coach's reply.

"Wow, that's the first one I've ever seen up close. It's beautiful!"

"Thanks. You never saw one ever before?" Jacques inquired.

"No, well actually, I'm a Leafs fan, so, I guess you'll laugh at me now. . . ."

Demers didn't laugh, but he was wearing a broad grin and just as the admirer opened the contents of his package, he began bellowing with roaring cackles.

"Where on Earth did you find that?" the coach was heard to ask.

"I made it myself!" said the man in his thirties.

"No way! That's so . . . I don't know what to say. I'm just . . . I'm lost for words! I've never seen anything like that in my life!"

By this time, the man and his friend were joined by a few other onlookers; yours truly having already been captivated close by. The item Demers focused his stunned gazed onto, sat before him, out of sight for others. Pale disbelief crossed the coach's facial expression, mixed with bursts of laughter.

"Serge! Boys, come and get a look at this!"

In a snap, the press box erupted with cacophonous hoots and snorts. Savard, grinning from ear to ear, took off his glasses for a closer look. Bert Raymond shook his head. Tremblay's shoulders bounced like a hot potato in a rumble seat on a gravel road. The second period was well under way, but spectators closest to this scene were now turned around and standing on the backs of their chairs

Q 13 2

SEC.   ROW   SEAT

CORNWALL
CIVIC COMPLEX

COLORADO
vs.
MONTREAL
CANADIENS

SUNDAY - 7:30 P.M.
SEPTEMBER 17, 1995

EXHIBITION GAME

The author's game ticket
for the first game in
Avalanche history.

to get a glimpse at what the commotion was all about. They still had not seen the subject of Demers's astonishment when he complied, tilting the item for all to see. What he shared truly was a one-of-a-kind creation.

It was a painted, pine and balsa wood carving of a casket, decorated in Montreal Canadiens colors, with Demers lying inside, resting in peace. The attention to detail was incredible, right down to the coach's grey suit, wire-rimmed glasses and trim moustache. It was about ten inches in length, three wide and two high. It was painted as a replica of the Habs' then-white home jerseys, with decal team logos on all four sides.

As it is not every day that one gets to glimpse at oneself resting peacefully in passing. Demers leaned toward the casket's creator, quizzing the ulterior motives behind the task of creating such a detailed piece. As the man explained it, the idea was little more than an amusing and friendly lark, coming from a Maple Leafs fan to the Canadiens coach. There was no harm intended whatsoever. The notion had crossed his mind after the Canadiens missed the playoffs the season prior, and the sculptor pursued the opportunity upon the announcement of the Habs' exhibition against the Avalanche in Cornwall. As the man explained it, "I just figured that any coach who misses the playoffs in Montreal is as good as dead!"

While that comment drew more laughter from those close by, the coach added to everyone's stitches, saying, "The worst part is, I want to keep it!"

"You can," said its creator, "I made it for you to have!"

"But I couldn't possibly. You must have put so much time, effort and work into it," the coach graciously offered, looking around nervously at those laughing with him, some possibly at him.

"But I want you to have it. There's another one that I made, but this one is the better one. This one is for you!"

Demers shook his head, still very much in disbelief. "It's okay? You really want me to keep it?" he asked again, still quite bemused. "Yes, yes. Keep it. Please!"

With that, the coach stood up, his arm lunging out for a gentlemanly handshake with the courteous Leafs fan. For those close by, it must have seemed like they had witnessed just about the oddest meeting ever between a coach and a rival teams supporter.

Tremblay, standing right next to Demers by this time, surely had no inclination whatsoever about his own immediate fate in the weeks to come. Demers handed him the casket to show to others in the booth.

If die-hard Canadiens fans place faith in such myths as "Forum Ghosts" they might be just as easily inclined to subscribe to other incantations such as voodoo, kewpie dolls and witching spells.

Demers would never again win another game as Canadiens coach, losing the first four games of the 1995-96 campaign. He'd be fired after the fourth loss along with Savard, who indignantly refused to fire his coach so early into the season. Demers was replaced by the rookie Tremblay, who stood closest to him in the press box when he accepted the gift from the Maple Leafs' fan.

All three men touched the "casket"!

9

1982 – 1999: HOW IT ALL WENT WRONG—THE DOWNSIDE OF RONALD COREY'S REIGN

The Harmonious Front Office

Hockey is a business. Most supporters who realize this still consider it a sport, first and foremost. Emotional fans, as Sam Pollock so famously noted, do not grasp the financial aspects. Money is a sport in itself; a race of sorts. There is activity involved in the business of making money that is sometimes sporting, and often not. The risks taken by ownership and management in operating a sports franchise often remove any semblance of sportsmanship and fair play. There are games that people play. Behind the scenes, there are other races, as people of judged performance competitively jockey for position. The survival instinct is a part of human nature. Inside every hockey organization, there are three kinds of employees: those working to retain their position; those hoping to improve upon their standing by moving up; and those who exist with the fear of being leapfrogged by underlings.

Personalities assuredly play into the mix. Senator Donat Raymond was never keen on Tommy Gorman, though it was obvious that he required his services to achieve success at a pivotal time in Canadiens history. Frank Selke and Dick Irvin saw eye to eye on most matters, until the kindly coach could no longer reel in the Rocket's unbridled passion for winning at all costs. Sam Pollock and

Scotty Bowman, certainly shared a mutual insight into what it took to win, but towards the end of their relationship, they also had a differences of opinion on how to ultimately achieve it.

It says something that 16 of the Canadiens' 24 Stanley Cup titles were won during a 34-year span during which the club's destiny was guided by Selke and Pollock. Humility and shyness were traits that often described both men, and neither sought to improve upon their position or was afraid for their standing. All they did was work incredibly hard, run a structured organization, and trust those working for them. They worked to win and win continuously, figuring the rest would take care of itself.

Pollock rarely, if ever, spoke of himself in terms of the accomplishment he had achieved while running the Canadiens. During his tenure, he was cornered once or twice for brief retrospective insights. Never one given to boasting, Pollock would only speak in a business management context regarding his Canadiens legacy. Queried within the perception of public opinion, he deflected all assessments of his achievement and legacy to money matters and bottom-line thinking. Fundamental business principles and practices, in Pollock's esteem, were akin to operating an animal farm. From the breeding to the selling off of assets, multiplication was the key. Accumulate numbers for starters, then quantify and plan forward. In his hockey analogy, his wisdom was as such: make sure the bills get paid; do what it takes to win; winning will take care of the bills. It was a no-nonsense business approach, which precluded any sort of outside perception. To that extent, he elaborated further, discussing winning and its inherent tradition. His words of wisdom practically became legend.

"Playing to the media or listening to the fans is the quickest way to start losing. Fans are great, but what they respect the most is a winner. The thing they know the least is managing a sports franchise. They have their favorites and strong emotional attachments to them. A sports administrator who wants to be successful can never think that way. You can never set out to build tradition. You start out to build a winner. If you can perpetuate that winner, you might end up with tradition. But tradition is a by-product. It can only be measured after the fact."

Pollock was indeed speaking after the fact, as the quote came prior to the Canadiens Cup win of 1986. Pollock was without doubt a visionary. He seemed to be warning all his successors that they were to be damned by fan expectation and tradition, should they follow the wrong course.

The Corey and Savard Regime Leads
the Canadiens Back to the Summit

Ronald Corey was first noticed by the Montreal Canadiens ownership during his directorship as the president of the Carling-O'Keefe brewery. In the general public's perception, he had garnered notoriety as the executive brainchild behind the brewery war with Molsons; Carling being the Quebec Nordiques' biggest sponsor while the club waged a most heated rivalry with the Canadiens. Corey had previously earned his reputation as a director on the board of governors of several companies. He was a man on the rise when the Canadiens snatched him away from the Nordiques.

When Corey was first brought on as Montreal's team president, there were two diverging opinions on his hiring. One told of a brilliant maneuver by Molsons, as Corey was perfectly suited to the challenge of righting the Canadiens' front office. There were however, concerns that Corey did not have a background as a hockey man in the purest tradition. The criticisms would vanish quickly, though, as soon as Corey replaced Grundman with Serge Savard, who then brought in Jacques Lemaire as assistant coach to Bob Berry. The Canadiens had never required a promotional and publicity department in the past, and one of Corey's initial moves was to hire a marketing firm to spruce up the manner in which the club presented themselves to their adoring fans. Corey also projected a hands-on approach for himself, taking a seat at the Forum directly behind the Canadiens bench.

Corey's hiring of Savard as GM was an experiment of sorts, and a nod to changing times. Former players, perhaps due to emotional attachment, did not always make for the best managers. Prior to Corey hiring Savard, the Canadiens had never had a former player manage the team, unless one counts Jack Laviolette, who acted as both player and manager in 1909-10. But as far as former players went, Savard was not your average athlete. Nicknamed "Senator" by his acolytes, Savard was extremely well read and worldly, mingling with politicians and stock brokers as well as with teammates. He built up a wealth of property investments that were paying off and was highly respected by all who knew him. Most importantly, his entire time in the Montreal organization had spanned the Pollock era, almost from beginning to end. Savard was a 17-year-old with Pollock's Junior Canadiens in 1963, becoming their captain the following season. Notoriously observant and astute, he had picked up on the mannerisms of Pollock and Bowman and combined this with his own experiences as a player.

Things did not begin well for the Corey-Savard regime. With seventeen games remaining in the 1983-84 season, the new GM dismissed Coach Bob Berry, replacing him with standby Lemaire. The coaching change seemed to have little influence in the regular season, but the 1984 playoffs, as is often the case, was another story altogether. Lemaire's tactics, combined with the surprising goaltending of Steve Penney, pushed the Canadiens three rounds deep. A miracle seemed to be playing itself out, when the Habs struck down the second overall Bruins in a three-game sweep and followed with a six-game upset of the heavily favored Nordiques. They had a 2-0 lead in games against the mighty Islanders, when the defending Cup champions got their act together and reduced the Canadiens to five goals in the final four games.

Despite the disappointing end to the 1984 season, spirits were revived, and the hiring of Corey, Savard and Lemaire combined to instill a greater faith all around. For the remainder of the decade, the Canadiens were in good hands. Regardless of the notion that many assets from the '70's dynasty had not provided for returns of equal quality, Savard drafted smartly and made well-informed moves to continuously strengthen the roster. As the Canadiens had won at least two Stanley Cups in every decade since the 1920's, there existed the perception that the Canadiens were no longer a hockey power in the '80s. While they did not measure up to previous high standards, they were not far off.

Throughout the 1980's, the Canadiens would manage to maintain their standing amongst the top NHL clubs. They remained strong regular season finishers from 1980 to 1989, apart from the

'84 campaign, in which they plummeted to a 75-point total. While there is but one title to show for the decade, they were the third-best club in the NHL during that time, finishing second overall twice, third three times and fifth on three occasions. They finished seventh overall in 1986, a year in which they would win the Cup, and eleventh in 1984, where they went on to play three rounds deep into the playoffs. They averaged 98.3 points per season during the decade, when only the Oilers (99.6) and the Flyers (99.2) were better. The playoffs presented another matter in the city used to championships. There is the perception of incredible failure arising from three seasons, '81 to '83, in which they did not win a round, but in total the Canadiens won 14 of 23 series they played, winning 67 of 115 games.

But success of any lesser kind does not pass the test in the esteem of many Montrealers, the media inclusive. Being simply good enough, or even among the better teams, requires a patience its supporters have never had the opportunity of learning. Nevertheless, the pressure to win was immense and the demands placed on those in charge took their toll. The Canadiens employed no less than six coaches in those ten seasons. All of Bernie Geoffrion, Claude Ruel, and Lemaire as well as Jean Perron and Pat Burns, had difficulty living up to the scrutiny or maintaining past standards. Bob Berry stuck around long enough to be fired twice within one year, and Jean Perron, after helping the team to the '86 Cup, was fired two seasons later.

Although the Canadiens had begun their rise back amongst the league elite, there remained an underlying sense of distress.

The Hockey Religion Meets the New Media

It is often mentioned that hockey in Montreal is akin to a religion of sorts. Books have been written on the topic. University courses taught in the city and in the province of Quebec have explored such a thesis, more than a few times. At the Université de Montreal in 2008, Professor Olivier Bauer's class expounded on this particular subject. A CBC news article covering Bauer's course began by imploring that "the arena is their temple, the players are their saviors, and those who worship them pray that the sacrifices made on

the ice of blood, sweat and tears will lead them to glory." Given such a heightened context, it can be understood that the players donning the Montreal Canadiens' colors are easily elevated to the status of idols, heroes and role models.

The Montreal hockey media is a unique microcosm, and the team's hockey fans are more akin to disciples than the average supporters. Hence, given these extreme parameters, the players are then held up to a higher, more divine light. The expectations placed upon the players are enormous. Based on the assessments of past legendary stars, it is no stretch to consider that some were seen as gods. Today, all of its players, from highly paid stars to role players, are deemed as servants to the past. Most of those skating for the team are required to be saints, at the very least. Mere mortals, all faults inclusive, can never live up. They are condemned to raise Stanley Cups above their heads or fail in comparison. Twenty-four Stanley Cup titles won have that effect.

The perception that continues to exist today was very much the team reality in the late 1980's. The players began making the news for matters unrelated to hockey. General Manager Serge Savard, who usually assumed a cool posture for the press when juggling hot potatoes, had become quite adept at putting out fires in recent years. Behind the scenes his plate was becoming fuller as the seasons ensued. Players were changing, in both attitude and personal complexity during the decade. Bigger salaries and a greater awareness of their stature as public figures and athletes of value had unshackled the players' free spirits. With this, and not uncoincidentally, fans and readers of hockey news were no longer satisfied with simple game summaries and highlight reel descriptions of goals. They now wanted to know about the players' lives outside the arena.

As matters evolved, this meant that GM Savard not only had to act in his usual hockey capacities, but he was also tasked with managing the public opinion regarding off-ice matters that made the newspapers. Also managing the public perception attached to the club was team President Ronald Corey, a marketing man by trade. Corey grew up in an era in which the players' personal lives were rarely reported upon. Those pulling on Canadiens' sweaters were revered idols in Corey's youth. His heroes could do no wrong, and if they had, it was certainly not reported in the papers.

Changing right along with the modern athlete was the media that covered all publicized aspects of sport. The advent of the twenty-four hour televised sports channel greatly altered the dynamic of the press. More news was needed to feed the immediacy of the new medium and in seeking additional storylines and alternate angles of reporting, the press began a practice of portraying players in an opposing light. The role model–the good guy— remained, but for want of a better term, some were now becoming painted as spoiled brats. The description did not always fit, and more often than not, was extremely misleading. Included in these portrayals, the players' off-ice indiscretions often came into play.

Oftentimes, the new media caught the club quite off guard, reporting on behavior that was anything but classy.

It's Hard to be a Saint in the City of Montreal

Montreal as a hockey city is renowned for several reasons. There is a winning tradition, unlike in any other city. There is the religious fervor of fans. There is the press horde, the daily media scrum before, after and between games. Added to all this, there are the nightlife temptations of a city that never sleeps. The lure of all that Montreal has to offer at every end of the entertainment spectrum often pulls players into unsaintly behavior.

During the latter part of the decade, this became an issue for management, as a series of minor incidents and negative player headlines set the wheels in motion for larger implosions. Several elements of combustion were forming under pressure, deceptively veiled behind the winning shrouds. Team management was reading of the media catching wind of several player escapades, and the magnitude of the growing whispers was largely concerning. They couldn't help but be aware of the circumstances, as it was reported to an increasingly upset fan base. The tales involved the nightlife habits of a half-dozen players that involved the usual concoction of late night drinking, women, the occasional bar scuffle and some vehicular scrapes and dentings.

The offenders, the club was informed, included a cast of characters repeatedly making the news for all the wrong reasons. Something had to be done about it.

147

The image-conscious Corey, always on the beat, couldn't have liked it much. Following each incident, a vow would be made to look into the details of each. To counter balance, Savard's wisdom was often quoted, as he was more willing to consider each matter as an isolated incident, reasoning that they were only doing what generations of previous Canadiens players had also done. Savard was not wrong in his view, yet he was concerned at the repeated nature of the claims involving the names of the same players over time.

In late April of 1988, only a few days after the Canadiens had been eliminated by Boston, a controversial story emerged in the Montreal press concerning three players breaking curfew during playoff time. Testament to the proportion of importance the Canadiens take on in the province, the story bumped meetings between Prime Minister Brian Mulroney and President Ronald Reagan on the issue of acid rain from the front pages of newspapers and dominated talk radio for days. Forty-eight hours prior to the first playoff game, the team was sequestered at a resort on Charron Island outside of Montreal. The players jokingly called it Alcatraz. As the story went, Coach Perron had done his usual 11 p.m. room checks, and every player was present and accounted for. He reportedly also had someone stationed at the front entrance in the event anyone tried to slip out.

As the tale reported in *La Presse* went, three players allegedly bribed a restaurant chef into allowing them to escape through the back kitchen door and out into the night. The restless trio then supposedly took a taxi to a late night eatery in town and was there only long enough to sip a couple beers before departing the scene with two women. As the group left the parking lot, the female driver had apparently bumped into another car before knocking over a lamp post. Before the police arrived, the players left the scene, supposedly beating a path straight back to the resort. Though a handful of witnesses had apparently described them as possible Canadiens players, they were not identified or mentioned in the police report. They were however, mentioned in the press. The entire affair would cause a big headache for the Canadiens organization and a mess for the local police force, who were perceived as giving the celebrity players a free pass from justice. In the esteem of many, the incident shamed the Canadiens organization.

When the incident first occurred, it seemed there was not much of a story to report. News of the car accident and details of the player indiscretions tying into the story did not make the papers until over three weeks after the fact, coming to light the day after the Canadiens had been eliminated from the playoffs. When the first reports hit the newsstands, there were many holes in the accounting of the tale. The police investigating the accident had not seen the players in question, nor were they mentioned by the driver of the vehicle. The chef who allegedly accepted the bribe was neither named nor quoted. Just as importantly, the exact date of the incident was prior to the Canadiens beginning their first-round playoff series against the Hartford Whalers, when it was unlikely that a curfew would have been imposed upon the players. If the incident happened on or about April 4, why had it not come to light until April 27?

An article by Francois Lemenu, published in *Le Devoir* the day after the story broke in *La Presse*, pointed to the inconsistencies in the story that had now become the talk of all of Montreal. The three players concerned were baffled by the reports and were defiant in their stance that nothing of the sort had happened. The article was quite detailed. Lemenu identified the players, the bar in question as being the New York, New York discotheque in Longueuil and also noted that the female driver had hit a parked car on Marie-Victoria Boulevard. Along with quotes from two of the players named, the piece also contained the exasperations of the parents of the two young women. In each case, the related testimonials Lemenu uncovered differed greatly from the seemingly sensationalist tale that had by then manifested itself into a full-blown controversy.

In the Canadiens' dressing room the day after elimination, one player involved threatened to smash a photographer's camera equipment as he prepared to snap a photo. The outraged defenseman was quoted as saying "None of this is true. It's a bunch of lies, likely perpetrated by a Nordiques fan." Another player was equally perturbed. "It makes no sense at all," he said. "It's a joke. How can they write such things—especially prior to a playoff game? It's ridiculous. In Montreal, it's always the same thing when the team losses. Each time, it seems journalists need to find a reason to explain why we lost."

Lemenu's article ends with the mother of the driver challenging that the information reported was inaccurate. The other parent demanded that the media cease involving her daughter in a story she was not part of. In short, none of the principals identified as being involved could certify that Canadiens players had anything to with the incident.

Could the entire story, as the defenseman suggested, have been a fabrication devised to sully the Canadiens' reputation?

This was no longer the tale of a car bumping a lamp post in a parking lot. It was the collision between the religion of hockey and the new methods of the media. The tempest in a teapot grew in proportion as the days ensued. By April 30, after much damage had been caused, reporters were writing of the incident in a sarcastic, mocking tone. In an article titled "The Three Sinners" by *Le Devoir's* Jean-Luc Duguay, the writer essentially castigates his own medium for the attention paid to the story. Things had gotten way out of proportion, Duguay related.

"To the more sensitive souls out there, it should be mentioned that such player escapades have been going on since the beginning of time. The boss of these three supposed sinners, Serge Savard, had admitted that when the glorious Canadiens of the seventies were busy collecting Stanley Cups, they too had found equally creative ways of slipping under Scotty Bowman's radar on a nightly basis. Like these latest bad boys, they assuredly hit town looking for a female or two, who would be interested in heading to the theatre where they could discuss Shakespeare's influence on modern film."

Savard was not a man who liked to fire his coaches. One of his first moves as GM in the summer of 1983 was to reinstate the fired Bob Berry behind the bench, while Jacques Lemaire was groomed for the intense task that would later be handed to him. The GM rationed that continuity and stability within the coaching ranks and on the team roster was crucial. In his experience, he had learned that it was best to deal players from a position of strength, and not when their value had been lowered by rumors of extracurricular incidents. Similarly, as it applied to his coaching staff, Savard also paused when his players threatened mutiny. Most of his own career was played under the rule of Scotty Bowman, whose contrarian tactics kept players on edge. Winning, and meeting expectations, were what matters most to managers of sports franchises, likely including Savard. If a scattering of players were displeased with Jean Perron's methods, it was par for the course. When half the team expressed antipathy, it was another matter altogether.

Immediately following the 1988 playoffs, rumors began to swirl that Perron's job was in jeopardy. Savard quickly extinguished that fire, reassuring his coach in the process. Despite the GM's proclamation however, the story would not die. One source for this was Mario Tremblay, the former player turned reporter, who claimed to have it on good authority that Perron would be replaced. At the onset, few gave Tremblay's assurances much merit. After all, it would be somewhat unprecedented for the Canadiens to nudge its bench boss off the plank so soon after a Stanley Cup win and following three regular seasons of improvement in the standings. The press defended the coach, as Savard had not yet even sat down with Perron to discuss the campaign. They were scheduled to meet, as usual, two weeks after the season ended.

Perron was ultimately dismissed, but as with any major hockey news in the city of Montreal, the story contained multiple wrinkles, all reported on in depth by the press. Upon returning from vacation, Perron was met by the microphones at the airport. When asked if he had handed in his resignation, the response was "You can get that idea out of your mind. I'll never quit." Four days later, after meetings with Savard, it was announced by the club that the coach had resigned. In the book *Robinson for the Defense*, the former Canadiens rearguard told that player discussions with Savard had swayed the manager's stance. In discussing his conditional return to the team for another season with Savard, Robinson put forth the unhappiness of the players as it concerned their coach. He thought of retirement, if Perron was not removed, and told that fellow defenseman Rick Green felt similarly. "I wasn't alone. Neither of us had been pleased with the 1987-88 season and all the turmoil and recriminations that upset the dressing room. Try as we might, along with Bob Gainey and other veterans like Smith, Walter and Carbonneau, we couldn't convince the team to play for the coach."

Some reports however, stated that Perron's firing was not solely the result of a disappointing season or a mutiny on the players' part. According to the coach himself, in interviews as late as 2009, the firing was a reaction by the Canadiens' front office to the lamp post incident. The coach's view stems from knowing that Tremblay had the scoop on the story, before his sit down with Savard. In an article by RDS's Jean-Paul Sarault titled *Fired...because of a lamp post,* the coach notes that "Before it happened to me, I didn't think it was possible to get rid of a coach after a 103-point season. I was after all, a coach-of-the year finalist. Before I left for my vacation, I talked contract with Serge Savard, who told me we would settle that up upon my return." Sarault then brings up the lamp post incident, noting how "the Canadiens' image was a sacred matter to then-team president Ronald Corey, who tolerated little in terms of player misbehavior." Perron bristles at this. "Here's the thing. That night, I checked all the rooms. What else was I to do? A coach cannot chain players to their bed posts overnight! After I was fired, for a time, I'd lost all desires to coach again."

While the lack of stability and continuity behind the bench was most concerning to him, Savard had indeed found a perfect successor in Pat Burns, hired one year earlier to man the Sherbrooke Canadiens farm club. After the Charron Island alleged indiscretions, Burns, the former Gatineau detective, became the perfectly suited candidate for the task at hand. He would reel in all violators of club rules and instill discipline, the media was told, before his de facto hiring became official. At his press conference, Burns stated flatly that he was hired based on his ability to win hockey games, rather than his cop qualifications. Less than twelve months later, Burns had guided the Canadiens to a 115-point finish, their strongest regular season showing since 1979. He won the Jack Adams Trophy as NHL coach of the year, voted on weeks before he guided the club into a six-game Stanley Cup Final loss to the Calgary Flames.

Having now replaced the coach, several players would soon be on the move as well. The first of these to go was enforcer John Kordic, whose fists of steel were reminiscent of the legendary John Ferguson. Savard sent Kordic to the Maple Leafs, who dangled the unphysical, but highly productive Russ Courtnall in return. The completed theft would turn out to be an upgrade of unforeseen proportion. Courtnall dazzled Montreal crowds for three seasons before falling out of favor with Burns. In the summer of 1993,

Courtnall was dispatched to Minnesota for 40-goal scorer Brian Bellows.

Cornerstone Chelios Departs in a
Savardian Spinnerama

Chris Chelios, winner of the 1989 Norris Trophy as the NHL's best defenseman, was next to go. On the Canadiens blue line for six seasons, Chelios proved to be a pillar of strength. Yet an off-the-ice incident in the summer of 1990 seemed to foreshadow his fate as a Canadien. While visiting family in Madison, Wisconsin in late June, Chelios was charged by local police with resisting arrest after he was allegedly observed urinating on a public street. The Canadiens organization dealt him to the Blackhawks the very next day.

Chelios was no stranger to such reports. As author D'Arcy Jenish tells in "*The Montreal Canadiens – 100 Years of Glory*", Chelios' "off-ice antics spawned a swirl of gossip and rumor. There were tales of an affair with the wife of a Canadiens executive, alleged dalliances with starstruck underage teens, and a fracas with a streetwalker. Reporters chased every story, but none of the rumblings were ever substantiated. Savard always reached with trepidation for his morning paper, half expecting that he would see his co-captain's picture beneath a scandalous headline." Jenish also relates that an unproven rumor had it that team president Corey had ordered the trade, fearing that Chelios' shenanigans would again embarrass the organization. This was a claim that Savard almost immediately denied.

In the ensuing days following the trade, Savard would offer details to a story he would stick to for years to come. As he put it, the team was more concerned about Chelios' recurring leg and knee injuries than his discipline at the time. The defenseman had missed twenty-seven games during the 1989-90 campaign, and though he had only missed nine games over the two previous years, Savard related that he had a specialist look over his star player's prognosis and the results were far from reassuring. As the GM explained it, doctors told that cumulative leg and knee injuries sustained by Chelios placed his prolonged career in jeopardy. He might last another five seasons, at best.

Few in the Montreal press questioned Savard on this. In the short term, the medical explanation made sense. Everyone had watched Chelios hobble through the previous season on a badly injured knee, and they reasoned that explanations added up. Few journalists, however, had rationed that Savard himself went on to win five Stanley Cups after suffering two broken legs. It was not an easy call for the GM to make. He loved Chelios as a player, later admitting the trade had not been a good one. Chelios went on to play seventeen more NHL seasons, retiring at age 48. The defenseman who became the second oldest active NHL player of all time turned into a fitness fanatic and completely altered his workout routines and training regimens following his trade from the Canadiens. Who could have known?

The Canadiens had performed up to expectations in the 1989-90 regular season. They finished fourth overall in the NHL standings, but third in a tight Adams Division race. They drew second-place Buffalo in the first round, upsetting them in six games before losing out to Boston, the eventual Cup finalists, in five games. The loss didn't sit well with angry fans who were becoming slightly put off by Coach Burns' defensive style.

The offseason began with the usual questioning in the local press on how to fix what ailed the club. With the Chelios prognosis seriously worrying the Canadiens, the inevitable rumbles soon hit the papers with articles insinuating that he might be traded. Reader response columns curiously did not think it a bad idea. Things became interesting when some scribes began speculating what Chelios could fetch on the trade market. Once it was tabled that Chicago star Denis Savard had been in constant discord over the last season with his coach and GM Mike Keenan, the idea of a switch was launched. When the trigger was finally pulled on the deal on June 29, Chelios was shocked and dismayed that the Canadiens would trade him. He thought he would play his entire career with Montreal.

The acquisition of the Hawks' Savard played over well with fans and media during the summer. Bringing the local boy home distracted discussion of why Chelios was dealt. One year into the trade, however, it appeared the Canadiens had been deceived. Three seasons earlier, Savard had registered a career-high 131 points. The player the Habs received had slowed considerably, good only for 59 points. Chelios meanwhile was back in full form, counting for 64 points. One year later he would lead Chicago to the Cup final and win the Norris Trophy in 1993. That same year, Savard tallied 50 points and was a virtual non-factor as the Canadiens won their 24th Stanley Cup.

No one could have known at the time of the trade that Chelios would go on to play for another ten years, never mind two full decades. What people might have been able to see and sense beforehand was that Denis Savard's career was on the down slide. In the two seasons prior to joining Montreal, he had in fact missed double the number of games Chelios had. He also had difficulty playing in Keenan's grinding system and was then expected to prosper under the stringent Burns.

Denis Savard was a player that in many respects had gotten away from the Canadiens in the 1980 draft. They had instead gone for consensus first overall choice Doug Wickenheiser. On a weaker Chicago club, Savard was able to move straight to the top of their depth chart, practically outplaying number-one center Tom Lysiak. In Montreal, the 19-year-old Wickenheiser was tasked with out-dueling the likes of centers Pierre Larouche, Pierre Mondou, Keith Acton, Doug Jarvis and Doug Risebrough. He'd never catch a break.

As fate would have it, in Savard's first NHL game, he registered two assists against Buffalo. Two nights later, he was at the Forum, and Ruel chose to not dress his youngster. Savard then went out and dazzled, scoring his first NHL goal and adding an assist in a Blackhawks win. Capping his night off, he was named one of the game's three stars. Savard now had four points in a pair of games while Wickenheiser had yet to play. The comparisons began there. Two seasons later, at 21, Wickenheiser was the center with the second-highest number of points on the team with 25-30-55 totals, behind Ryan Walter, and ahead of Acton and Guy Carbonneau.

In the short term, the Chelios for Savard deal did not harm the Canadiens much. Several media men liked to point out that Chelios had been ably replaced in the team hierarchy by the likes of Eric Desjardins, Patrice Brisebois and Mathieu Schneider, but such is a disingenuous claim considering Chelios added to those three defensemen would have made the Canadiens all the better. Other writers took the angle that Chelios never helped lead Chicago to a Cup, whereas Savard had been a member of the '93 champion Canadiens. That claim did not seem to take into account the fact that Savard registered a mere five assists in fourteen playoff games, and was sidelined for the entire Stanley Cup Final. He assisted Demers as an associate coach behind the bench. Savard was set loose by the Canadiens following the Cup win and signed as a free agent with Tampa Bay. What the Canadiens could have accomplished by retaining Chelios is inestimable.

Yet this seemed to be just the start of a flood of transactions that would occur within the organization over the course of the next decade.

Bon Cop, Bad Cop

Pat Burns accomplished a feat during his Canadiens tenure that no Montreal coach preceding him in the previous decade or any coach since has managed: he lasted a full four seasons on the job. That he did so without being fired may be testament to Savard's belief in stability. Burns, an excellent coach, was an interesting study behind the bench. Animated mannerisms, facial expressions and exaggerated gestures made him a favorite of television cameras, and no one watching him had to wonder very long what was going through his mind or coming out of his mouth. Players knew exactly where they stood with the boisterous Irishman who held nothing back, and the media enjoyed his colorful descriptions of events the morning after games.

Under Burns, the Canadiens became even more defensively accountable, finishing either first or second in goals against in his four seasons behind the bench. He got great results out of marginal players, pushing them to exceed themselves, and he kept the egos of the star players grounded to a fault. Burns, however, had a difficult time reeling in his emotions on occasion. His patience with certain players wearing thin, he would be queried on their game play. An exasperated Burns would take a deep breath, gather his thoughts, puff out his cheeks, and speak his mind. He was notoriously harsh in regard to players such as Svoboda, Lemieux and Stephane Richer. If Burns had indeed been hired to police the Canadiens' wilder spirits, the results were negligible at best. A stream of off-ice shenanigans kept Burns and the Canadiens' brass on constant alert.

Upon Burns' death in 2010, the *Toronto Star*'s Mike Zeisberger shared his favorite stories of the coach, some painting a softer side of the ex-cop. It included a December 14, 1990 incident in which the coach was "snapped out of a deep sleep by a call informing him that three of his players—Mike Keane, Shayne Corson and Brian Skrudland—were behind bars. It seems [the] trio had been involved in a brawl at a Winnipeg watering hole, a development that angered the former cop. After bailing out his players and giving them a tongue-lashing, Burns found out the three had come to the aid of a man who had been badly roughed up. Burns quickly changed his tune and gave his players advice. While the three were charged with causing a disturbance by fighting, they were not convicted. 'That was Pat,' former Canadiens wing Kirk Muller said. 'When you needed something, the first guy who would call you was Pat.'"

In the early 1990's, Savard made several high-profile trades that rank among his best and worst. Sending Richer to New Jersey for Muller and Corson to Edmonton for Vincent Damphousse are among his most deft moves, while dealing Lemieux to Jersey for Sylvain Turgeon and sending Brian Skrudland to Calgary for Gary Leeman did not pay off. The deal for Denis Savard had not generated the expected boost in offense, and the GM was in continuous search for a more productive roster. When one finally materialized, Burns was no longer behind the bench,

Burns abruptly resigned from the Canadiens three weeks after their elimination in May 1992. Much of the criticism levied at him dealt with his team's lack of offensive creativity. His charges had dropped three successive playoff series to the Bruins, and the media were calling for his dismissal. He scowled at journalists' questions intoning that he'd been pushed to resign by Savard. The GM even denied the claim himself, noting that he had extended Burns' contract for two more seasons at a $400,000 salary. His replacement behind the bench would be Jacques Demers, a two-time Coach-of-the-Year winner who had been working as an analyst for Nordiques' games since being fired by Detroit in 1989.

Demers was a good guy with a good word for everyone he crossed paths with. He'd had a troubled life as a youngster, but hard work had taught him all the virtues he would require to make his way in life. He was an expressively grateful man for every positive turn his life had taken. No one knew at the time that Demers was functionally illiterate, but he had found ways around that setback like everything else. Preaching constant positivism and belief in oneself, he allowed players to play their games without much barking. He was a well-liked personality that everyone easily cheered for. Most importantly for the players, he did not have Burns' hardened exterior and coached a more wide open game. At the press conference unveiling him as the Canadiens' newest bench boss, he seemed absolutely star-struck and beside himself, noting the great Canadiens tradition innumerable times. To no one's surprise, he promised a more offensive club and indeed delivered on that promise.

Demers' first season behind the Canadiens' bench was a serendipitous tale. The Canadiens increased their scoring in 1992-93, from 267 to 326, thanks in no small part to the added contributions of Damphousse (39 goals) and Brian Bellows (40 goals), acquired in the off-season. They finished sixth in the league with a solid 102 points but went from first to seventh defensively, allowing 280 goals, 73 more than the previous season. Deceptively, their nine-point improvement on the regular season resulted in a drop from first to third place in the strong Adams Division. In the process of becoming a more offensive team, the focus shifted from the defensive aspects of the game. Goal scoring was up league-wide, but in the microcosm that is sometimes Montreal, the trend reflected poorly on goalie Patrick Roy.

Two seemingly innocuous events on the season conspired to place Roy in a bad light. Backup goalie Andre Racicot, the bulk of his games coming against weaker clubs, was outplaying Roy statistically. Fans had begun chanting his name whenever Roy allowed a soft goal. Prior to the season, Roy, an avid hockey card collector, signed on as a spokesperson for Upper Deck trading cards. Someone with a captive imagination in the company's marketing department brainstormed that a billboard with the phrase "Trade Roy!" would help spark sales. Unfortunately for Roy, it perversely ignited thought among fans that the Canadiens should do just that. Polls to that effect became prominent in newspapers, with several results calling for Racicot to be made the team's starter come playoff time. The issue of Roy's play became a constant question for Demers, who handled matters diplomatically, but chose his words badly in coming to Roy's rescue.

Demers, wanting to bolster his goalie's confidence while showing the public he had ultimate faith in his stopper's abilities, got into a comparison game with superstar athletes from other sports known for rising to the occasion. Perceiving Roy as a leader capable of carrying his team, he name dropped, among others, legendary NFL quarterback Joe Montana and basketball icon Michael Jordan. As the coach worded it, his goalie's performances were key to victory, which was certainly not off the mark, but the well-intentioned comparisons made it seem as though winning started, passed through and ended with the goalie. Roy was no ball carrier or quarterback; he was a large piece of the winning puzzle, along with many other equally important pieces. The players surrounding Roy in the dressing room, whose contributions were crucial to his success, wanted their share of attention and accolades. After the 1993 Stanley Cup, Demers' words glorifying Roy elevated the goalie to deity status, but the coach's proclamations regarding his stopper would have an adverse effect going forward.

Irreparable Collateral Damage

The 1993 Canadiens' Cup win was one for the ages. For the NHL, the Conference Finals presented a dream setup, with both series playing out in four of its largest markets. There was the dramatic Toronto and Los Angeles series out west, with the New York Islanders and the surprising Canadiens in the east. The storylines were thick and loaded with plot twists. Hockey's oldest and most storied franchises both appeared as teams of destiny. The Islanders, in upsetting Mario Lemieux and the defending champion Pittsburgh Penguins, were in the process of returning some shine to their tarnished franchise. Perhaps most importantly for league exposure, all eyes were on the continued exploits of the incredible Wayne Gretzky. The game's greatest player at the time was playing some of the most inspired hockey of his career. Hockey fans worldwide were elated when Gretzky and the Kings made it to the ultimate showcase against the overtime beasts that were Roy and the Canadiens.

Once the final was over, fans had witnessed Roy at the peak of his prowess, relegating a miserable and controversial regular season into a distant afterthought. The Canadiens' record-setting ten consecutive overtime wins etched into hockey lore, the conquests quickly became part of the Roy mystique and legend. With his second Conn Smythe win, Roy was now considered amongst the greatest goalies the game had seen. He now belonged in a sentence with Jordan and Montana. Demers' earlier words to that regard became prophecy. Roy was now a world-class winner in a city that transcends those not so merely mortal into deities. The disproportionate focus on the goalie's achievements sometimes pushed aside the combined accomplishments of some twenty or so players, seven of whom scored ten overtime goals. Roy-mania had been unleashed, and over the course of a couple of seasons, the pressure inherent in such heightened expectations would come back to harm both the player and the franchise.

The height of Roy-mania occurred near the time of what is perhaps his greatest game on April 25, 1994. The defense of the Canadiens Cup title began in Boston, with the Bruins owning home ice advantage for the playoff series. The Habs lost the first game before evening the series and returning to Montreal. After the second game, Roy had complained of soreness and sharp pains in his side. Visions of a second Cup in a row came crashing down when an examination revealed that Roy would need to have an emergency appendectomy. Doctors stated that the goalie would miss two weeks if they operated but they hoped to treat the infection intravenously with antibiotics over a two-day period. Ron Tugnutt, acquired in a one-sided trade for the snazzy Stephan Lebeau in February, was thrust into the starter's role. He fizzled in a 6-3 loss while Roy rested.

On the morning of April 23, Roy, ahead of doctors' evaluation of his condition, declared himself ready for action. Most doubted that Roy would be well enough to play, but rumors swirled throughout the day that he would indeed be between the pipes. Excitement in the city grew to a feverish pitch, and the Forum erupted come game time when Roy skated out to his crease. Carried in the rush, the Canadiens skated out to a 3-0 lead before the game was 12 minutes old. They would win the contest 5-2 to tie the series, but the real story of the game involved the adrenalized Roy holding off the desperate Bruins as they outshot Montreal by a 41 to 15 margin.

As good as Roy was in Game Four, he was absolutely wired two nights later. Back in Boston, the Canadiens wrestled the series lead away from the Bruins with a 2-1 overtime win. Roy stood on his head, both elbows and his aching appendage to stop 60 of 61 shots. All of La Belle Province was euphoric for Game Six, but the manic state was short-lived. The Canadiens lost 3-2, and the Bruins closed out the series in Boston on April 29. Testament to Roy-mania's lasting effect, when the goalie finally underwent surgery on May 3, it was claimed that someone associated with the hospital had kept the appendix as a hockey souvenir. The next day's papers told that they had received bids offering thousands of dollars for the appendage. Only in Montreal!

The city and province were still in the midst of sorting through their emotional grief over the Canadiens' early ouster from the playoffs when a full-blown controversy erupted centering on the team captain. Guy Carbonneau, an outspoken sort, was considered by the press to be a great interview when times were tough. He took on Demers late in the season for his over-praising of Roy at the expense of other worthy teammates and had become notorious for sticking up for rookies in the press.

Three days fresh from their elimination, the captain, along with Roy and Damphousse, were out playing a round of golf when they were spotted by representatives from *Le Journal de Montreal.* Hoping for an interview, members of the paper approached Carbonneau and the others. It is at this point in the story where versions of events begin to differ. The player explained that he and his cohorts begged off any notions of a quick chat, asking that their privacy be respected. No player, freshly eliminated, wants to discuss matters so soon after or have his picture taken on a golf course of all places. The paper's reps seemingly understood as much, the captain related. According to Carbonneau, they were all joking together as he continued up course after his tee off. As a lark, Carbonneau said, he gamely gave the photographer the finger. The paper's version, however, told of an irked player becoming confrontational upon seeing the photographer and journalist. There was no joking around at all, the paper claimed, as insults and threats were hurled. Once the captain was a safe distance away, he turned to them and flipped the bird. Normand Pichette's photograph of Carbo's middle digit was on the cover of *Le Journal* the next morning.

Ronald Corey, "forever hypersensitive when protecting the Canadiens' image" according to *Gazette* journalist Jack Todd, must have done a double-take seeing the morning paper. Carbonneau's actions, no matter how trivial, could not be pardoned by the team or explained away with a simple apology. Subsequently, Savard and the team issued a standard "we will deal with this internally" memo to the press in order to suppress the uproar. The fact that he did not immediately support his captain was concerning. His days in Montreal were numbered.

Carbonneau was the thinking man's hockey player, a defensive strategist in the mold of Bob Gainey. He was a three-time winner of the Frank Selke Trophy as the league's best defensive forward between 1988 and 1992. As a long-time veteran and captain, he was the lone remaining player on the roster with enough clout to put Roy in his place when needed. He brought intangibles to the Canadiens' dressing room such as leadership, experience and soul, but with one seemingly frustrated gesture, he was deemed expendable. Though he had much quality hockey left in him, he was dealt away that August for Jim Montgomery. Describing the trade, Todd colorfully termed the blunder as "a full-scale header off the diving board into an empty pool."

The elements that the Canadiens had purged from their team now included a Norris Trophy winner, a Selke Trophy winner, a Coach of the Year winner and finalist, a future Conn Smythe Trophy winner, the two co-captains and several gritty players. The Canadiens would continue to replace players of the blood, sweat and tears mould and in doing so appeared to dilute the soul of the hockey club one piece at a time.

In the lockout-shortened campaign of 1994-95, the Canadiens panicked uncharacteristically early. With goal scoring numbers down, they dealt forward Gilbert Dionne, dependable defenseman Eric Desjardins and the unexplainably disappointing John Leclair to the Flyers for Mark Recchi, a stocky sparkplug putting up great numbers in Philadelphia. When that move failed to ignite the Canadiens' offense sufficiently, they compounded the error late in the season by sending newly named captain Kirk Muller and Mathieu Schneider to the Islanders for the wholesome French superstar Pierre Turgeon and the enigmatic Vladimir Malakhov.

GM Savard, in all his moves, appeared to be trying to change team chemistry. It is common in team sport to cleanse a dressing room of players no longer wanting to be there. Dionne and Schneider had both incurred Roy's wrath; the former for pointing out that Roy had his defensemen scurrying about like headless chickens and the latter for backing up the claim that Demers was coaching based on the goalie's recommendations. Sports Illustrated's Michael Farber, in a December 18, 1995 piece, noted that the goalie was "happiest as coach-without-port-folio under Jacques Demers, who let Roy set his own schedule and all but kissed his most important asset." Savard, in retrospect, felt his error in making many of his trades was in not acting sooner, when the room first fractioned. By the time of the beginning of the 1995-96 season, the roster had been pillaged of even more character elements, all that remained from the core of the '93 Cup were Roy, Damphousse, newly named captain Mike Keane, Patrice Brisebois and battling rearguard Lyle Odelein. A disaster loomed on the horizon.

After unforgivably missing the playoffs in the lockout-shortened 1994-95 season and then impacting the tragedy by losing the first four games the following year, supporters were up in arms and the media was calling for changes. What they might not have expected was the wholesale organizational purging brought on by Corey so quickly into the season. For failing to make the postseason and losing four additional games, Corey sacrificed the whole of the coaching staff, several layers of management including Savard, most of the scouting department and eventually the franchise goalie.

Leading up to the events of early October and those in the first week of December, there were two mounting issues within the organization. The first involved Savard himself. Following the Cup win, he had spoken a few times about the upcoming end of his tenure as GM. He did not speak specifically of his intentions beyond a three-year timeframe, but some in the media claimed that he had his eyes on the Canadiens' presidency. In one instance of such a claim being reported, a follow-up piece appearing shortly after stated that Corey had no intentions of vacating his position anytime soon. When

Savard later stated that he wished he'd acted sooner in the Recchi and Turgeon trades, word came, veiled through the media, that he was divesting himself too much with other interests to the detriment of the Canadiens' needs. Corey and Savard were not seeing eye to eye and after the playoff miss and the terrible start to the 1995-96 schedule, and fans were calling for change. 29 months after his second Stanley Cup victory, Savard lost his job.

The other burning issue had to do with Patrick Roy. Management felt that his conduct and demeanor had become detrimental to the team. Savard later told that he was working on trading Roy to Colorado for a package that included Owen Nolan when he was fired, however the organization rationed that a coaching change was the simplest method of rectifying issues.

That Corey tossed his coach and manager in the same sweep is curious, in that this manner of organizational restructuring was not at all that unprecedented for him. When Corey arrived with the Canadiens in 1983, the first major shakeup he delivered was the firing of GM Grundman and Coach Berry. He hired Savard as his manager, although he had no NHL front office experience. Jacques Lemaire was brought in as an assistant coach, though his experience behind the bench was minimal. For four seasons, Lemaire essentially educated himself in different hockey programs, first in B League hockey in Sierre, Switzerland, then as an assistant in an NCAA program in Plattsburgh, New York, and most recently with Longueuil of the QMJHL. Both Savard and Lemaire were somewhat inexperienced in terms of working NHL positions, but it was the composite backgrounds of the men themselves that allowed for their ultimate success. What Corey saw were two men, acquainted as both former teammates and friends, and marinated in the great Canadiens' winning tradition.

So it was no surprise that Corey followed a similar pattern to bring in the loyal Réjean Houle as GM and his equally inexperienced friend Mario Tremblay as coach. In many ways, Houle was no more experienced than Savard upon his hire. Though Houle worked for the Molson organization for a decade, he had never held a hockey position, other than alumni president, at the time of his hire. Tremblay, like Lemaire, had no specific NHL coaching experience on his resume. While Tremblay had the profile of a potentially good coach, the distinction lost was in how Lemaire had schooled himself for the job. Tremblay was a television commentator at the time. Corey saw absolutely no reason why things could not work out a second time. Even the ticking time-bomb that was the impending Roy scenario had a similar precedent in the Guy Lafleur coerced retirement of 1984. The Canadiens, under Corey, had rebounded from that particular controversy to win their 23rd Stanley Cup fourteen months later.

Corey's moves appeared genial, albeit only temporarily, as Tremblay won his first six games behind the bench, an exploit achieved by no other first-year Habs coach. From there, though, it was all downhill, as the defining moment of the Houle-Tremblay regime came barreling at them only 42 days into their apprenticeship. Roy and Tremblay appeared to butt heads almost from the very beginning. Though both men made conscious efforts to work together for the good of the team, it soon became obvious that they were too much alike for sparks not to fly.

The lines were quickly drawn: Tremblay sought to establish himself as the lone voice in the dressing room, preaching a set of team rules to restore order, discipline and respect among the players; Roy agreed to concentrate solely on stopping pucks. Everyone was to be treated equally, regardless of stature or tenure. That directive did not last long. Soon, a rookie on the team showed up late for practice and was banished to the press box for that evening's game. A few nights later, Vincent Damphousse overslept and showed up for the Detroit game ten minutes before the warm-up was scheduled to start. Tremblay, arguing that Damphousse was needed to win the game, broke his own rule and allowed him to play. His reasons for sidestepping his own rules were personal, and the decision didn't go over well with Roy and captain Keane.

The night of December 2, 1995 will forever remain acidly etched in Canadiens lore, for both its fans and those of its rivals. The 11-1 loss is in the record books as the Canadiens' worst-ever Forum ice defeat. When all was said and done, it was the day in which the franchise pillars crumbled to reveal great layers of instability. It was the precise moment in which the Canadiens' present separated with its glorious past.

In the previous day's papers, Tremblay had allowed for some of his personal grievances to get in the way of the better interests of his team. *SI*'s Farber stated that "less than a week before his blowup with Roy, Tremblay told reporters how much he had chafed under Bowman. The irony is, when challenged by Roy in a game against Bowman's Red Wings, Tremblay responded exactly as Bowman might have." Tremblay wanted to beat Bowman badly, and vice versa. The teams prepared their game plans in consequence. Facing the powerful Detroit squad the next night, Tremblay's charges were a disorganized mess on the ice from the moment the puck was dropped. Bowman's strategy was quickly evident: he would play only his top two lines. The Red Wings scored three power play goals in the first frame to take a 5-1 lead into the intermission. A five-minute major courtesy of a Brisebois crosscheck gave Detroit the man advantage to start the second.

Tremblay decided not to replace Roy in net. Roy, with the team before him totally out of step, figured his coach would save him the embarrassment. Tremblay thought his goalie should continue the fight. In deciding not to pull Roy, Tremblay seemed to be setting his goalie up for humiliation in front of the hometown fans. The facial expression worn by the coach that night seemed to suggest that if that was the case, so be it. – Roy would learn who is boss! It was a rookie mistake made by a coach unaware of the tangle of circumstances.

Midway through the second period, Roy allowed a ninth goal. His teammates had seemingly abandoned him, and now the fans were all over him. In the face of their derision, he raised both arms in a mock salute. The goalie, now broken down, was yanked from the game.

Tremblay stood at the bench, arms folded in defiance. Roy entered the area, tossed some equipment pieces in the hallway and proceeded past the coach to his spot at the end of the bench. Tremblay was glaringly silent, his chin authoritatively raised and Bowman-like as Roy passed by. With steam coming out his ears, Roy immediately turned to walk past Tremblay to Corey's ill-fated front row seat. There, he informed the president that he was done as a Montreal Canadien. Without hearing a word of this, hockey fans watching everywhere sensed the same.

Roy tried the next day to take the moment back, but to no avail. The Canadiens decided that his gestures were behavior unacceptable of a member of the team. In a private meeting, he was told he would be traded as soon as possible. The next day, a red-eyed Roy apologized to the team's fans. The situation was irreconcilable. As Farber put it, "Canadiens president Ronald Corey and new Montreal general manager Réjean Houle made sure Roy was not a coach killer by backing Tremblay."

On December 6, the Canadiens made the trade official. Roy was now a member of the Colorado Avalanche, with 20-year-old goalie Jocelyn Thibault and forwards Martin Rucinsky and Andrei Kovalenko coming to Montreal. In one final concession to tradition, Captain Mike Keane, who had earlier in the season declared that he felt no need to learn French, was also thrown in the deal.

It could have all been handled much differently, certainly much better, but with Roy now gone the Canadiens had lost their last remaining link to greatness.

The Forum Ghosts Didn't Make the Trip

For several years now, Corey had been charged with overseeing the Canadiens' move from the iconic Montreal Forum into the new Molson Centre, located a few blocks away. The edifice was grand in every conceivable way, and in being entrusted by club owners to deliver a new hockey shrine to Montrealers, Corey did not disappoint. The building was magnificent but still needed to find the soul that made it tremble. That would take some time.

It was often said that the Forum had many ghosts, and that those spirits of former players deceased – Vezina, Morenz, Newsy and others – were the home ice advantage behind every bounce and rut in the ice that favored the Canadiens. Lavish ceremonies were planned in the celebrated move from the Forum to the newer residence, but would the "ghosts" make their way as well?

Tradition, as Sam Pollock so long ago advised, was not an achievable concept in itself. Winning came first. The Canadiens sometimes acted as though tradition was a recipe. After Roy and Keane were traded to Colorado, the team named Pierre Turgeon as its captain. In the ceremonies planned for the move from the Forum to the Molson Centre, the final symbolic gesture was a carrying of the Habs' proverbial torch, from old shrine to new. The Canadiens' oldest living captain was Emile Bouchard. Butch also happened to be the first French-Canadian captain in team history, going back to 1948. With Turgeon wearing the "C" and holding the flame high above his head, the building would close with the team once again having a French-Canadian leader. He had been a Canadien for exactly 83 games.

Players the likes of Roy, Keane, Carbonneau, Muller, Schneider, Desjardins, Lemieux, Richer, Skrudland, Chelios and Corson could have been part of those closing ceremonies. As members of the last two Stanley Cup teams, some certainly deserved the honor. The Montreal Forum closed its doors as a hockey shrine on March 11, 1996. In the final game it hosted, the Canadiens beat Dallas by a score of 4-1. Andrei Kovalenko scored the final Forum goal, adding two assists in the game.

Far away from the hockey cameras on this night, grinding fourth-line forward Turner Stevenson had ideas all his own on how to mark the moment. Well after the ceremonies had ended, Stevenson walked back out onto Forum ice, metal scoop in hand. Scraping into the hardened ice, he chiseled a bag filled with frozen Forum ice chips. Five days later at the Molson Centre, well before Turgeon carried the torch inside, Stevenson poured water from the melted chips onto the ice of his new home.

As fate would have it, Stevenson scored the first-ever goal celebrated in Molson Centre history, only to have it disallowed.

The ghosts didn't make the trip.

10

1999-2012: AFTER THE WILDERNESS, HOPE

The Spin Cycle

In November of 1998, the team parted ways with goaltender Jocelyn Thibault, still a young and valuable asset at age 24, and sent him to Chicago with Dave Manson for goalie Jeff Hackett and defenseman Eric Weinrich. The deal was described as youth for experience, as it had been decided that the team required more leadership from proven veterans to move forward. GM Rejean Houle's Canadiens had yet to miss the playoffs in three seasons under his watch and they had won their first postseason series since 1993 the previous spring. In his esteem, this was a hockey club on its way back to the top. Come March, it appeared as if there had been a reversal of philosophy, as arguably the team's best two players in Captain Vincent Damphousse and forward Mark Recchi had been traded. It now seemed the club needed to get younger again.

It appeared that what Houle was really up to was unloading the team's highest salaried players. The Canadiens were in a financial mess, and it came to hamper the hockey operations. On the way to their worst regular season in over 50 years, the Habs were unbelievably bleeding money, to the tune of close to four million dollars per year in losses. The spiraling value of the Canadian dollar at the time had caused the franchise to become both uncompetitive and unprofitable.

News soon came that both the club and the Molson Centre were up for sale. Ronald Corey called it a day. Within a year new president Pierre Boivin cleaned house, and Houle and coach Alain Vigneault were shown the door. Ownership changed hands in 2001, when American George Gillette purchased the Molson Centre and an 80.1 percent share of the team. There were initial worries that Gillette could potentially move the club to the United States, but he held firm to promises that such a notion was unthinkable.

Although the Canadiens would miss the playoffs for three straight years, Gillette's influence on the club was a stabilizing one. In what were some of the franchise's darkest times, he never panicked, and the team slowly began turning the corner back to respectability. He allowed Boivin and his men to be secure in their positions despite the club's trials, and soon that calm approach paid dividends. Following the 2001-02 campaign, new GM Andre Savard lured former Ottawa Senators' scouting compatriot Trevor Timmins to head the Canadiens' scouting department. It would prove to be a sound move. Since the millennium, there have been three regime changes in the Canadiens front office in a dozen years, and Timmins has outlasted each.

There have been many peaks and valleys, controversies, trials and near tragedies since 2000. The Millennium almost began with a death on Molson Centre ice on January 29, when forward Trent McCleary, diving to block the puck, took a point shot from the Flyers' Chris Therrien directly in the throat, fracturing his larynx and collapsing his lung. Unable to breathe, he quickly skated to the Canadiens bench and lost consciousness in the hallway. Doctors saved his life right where he lay by opening an airway that allowed him to regain oxygen. Although it was virtually assured McCleary would never play again, the Canadiens, in a classy move by Gillette, signed him to a one-year contract the following summer. After a difficult training camp proved he couldn't continue, the team kept him on as a Western League scout.

Koivu's Inspired Return Provides the
Molson Centre with a Soul

The Canadiens returned to the playoffs at long last in 2002, but not without the trials and great courage displayed by Captain Saku Koivu.

Drafted in 1993, Koivu initially showed limitless potential, but soon a series of injuries would curb his ability to be the player he could've been. Koivu played a no-holds-barred style at both ends of the rink, putting his nose to the grindstone in every puck battle. Far from an imposing presence, the diminutive Finn was nonetheless a heart and soul player who left everything on the ice. Two knee surgeries and a dislocated shoulder were the result of his style of play, but he was, when healthy, one of the most committed players on the team.

In 1999, he was named captain, which did not please the French press, which continued its tired mantra that the Canadiens' captain should speak their language. That nonsense was quickly cast aside when it was discovered prior to the 2001-02 training camp that Koivu had cancer. He was diagnosed with Burkitt's lymphoma, a rare form of stomach cancer. Arriving on a plane flight from Finland with teammate Brian Savage, Koivu looked pale and complained of stomach pains. His illness soon progressed to vomiting, and as soon as he landed in Montreal he had an appointment with team physician Dr. David Mulder. Tests soon confirmed that Koivu was inflicted with a form of non-Hodgkin's lymphoma. Almost immediately, Koivu began undergoing treatment. When the Canadiens announced the news in a press conference, the entire hockey world went into shock.

Mulder delivered a positive side to the odds of beating the illness. Though it was a rare form of lymphoma, it was beatable with a better than 50 percent success rate. What Koivu had going for him was that he was young, strong and otherwise healthy. Yet the doctor stressed that the illness was indeed life threatening, and would not discuss how it compromised his career should he survive. On the whole, despite the grim outlook, the prospects for a complete recovery for a person of Koivu's stripe were encouraging.

The media cast gloom on the Canadiens' forthcoming season. A nonplayoff team even with Koivu at his best, few gave Montreal a chance to make the postseason without him. Behind the scenes, however, Koivu was not only determined to defeat the illness, but also he set a goal for himself to return before the playoffs. Mulder, who did not want to discourage his patient, also didn't want Koivu pushing himself too hard only to encounter disappointment and a possible setback. The media allowed Koivu his privacy as he underwent treatment, and the team gave regular updates on his progress. When the season began, Coach Michel Therrien proclaimed that he would not appoint an interim captain.

The Canadiens started the season strong, winning three of four before hitting a ten-game skid where they won only once. Seeming to sense a void in leadership, Savard signed NHL great Doug Gilmour, then in the twilight of a long career. In only his second game in a Habs uniform, Gilmour came to the defense of a player who had been assaulted in a game in Buffalo. Tossed from the game and suspended, Gilmour, however, left the message that certain gestures would not be tolerated. His attitude bolstered the team, which went on to win its first game in four contests. Not long after Gilmour returned, the compete level on the club was raised by more than a few notches.

Another compelling story of the 2001-02 season was the play of 25-year-old goaltender Jose Theodore. Playing in only his second full season as the Canadiens' starter, he posted incredible numbers as the Habs were involved in close games all season long. He finished with a 2.11 goals against average and .931 save percentage. At season's end, he was awarded both the Vézina Trophy and the Hart Trophy as League MVP. He was especially stellar down the stretch, allowing a frugal eight goals in seven games as the Canadiens battled for a playoff spot.

By mid-March, with the Canadiens in a dog fight for the playoffs, it was announced that Koivu had completed treatment and had now begun training for a potential return. The news was beyond belief, and without a doubt inspired the team. Anticipation built as Koivu progressed and began working out with teammates late in the month. As he neared his return, the Canadiens got hot, winning six in a row. The stage was then set. On April 9, in the third-to-last game of the season, with the team needing a win to clinch a playoff position, Koivu made his return against the same Ottawa Senators that Montreal had defeated two nights earlier.

The scenario had the Bell Centre crowd in a frenzy as it cheered Koivu throughout every stride of his pregame skate. Hundreds of charged-up fans carried homemade posters and placards welcoming the captain back and wishing him love and wellness. The atmosphere inside the building was surreal, and it soon became apparent that the Bell had never rocked as hard. When Koivu was announced as one of the game's starters, the emotion swelled to a feverish pitch. Montrealers then gave Koivu an ovation the likes of which they'd only ever reserved for Maurice Richard. And Koivu merited every ounce of it.

That the Canadiens then went out and defeated Ottawa 4-3 to clinch a playoff seemed almost anticlimactic. The building, alive as it had never been before, practically willed the win from the team. In the aftermath, Gillette spoke of an unparalleled achievement in sports. Gilmour, who had seen a few things in his time, described Koivu's achievement, the ovation he received, and the intensity of the game itself as one of the most amazing things he'd witnessed as a hockey player.

Following the memorable contest, Bertrand Raymond from *Le Journal de Montreal* sat with Dr. Mulder, in order to better comprehend the depth of Koivu's achievement. Mulder did not wish to go on record, but Raymond felt the story needed telling.

"The miracle isn't that Saku is alive," said Mulder. "It is that he is already back playing. The draconian regime which he imposed on himself in order to make it back and play surpasses everything I've ever seen."

Mulder admitted to the paper that he feared Koivu returning too soon.

"In each case," Mulder said, "I set the bar much higher than I normally would."

In order to return to the ice, Koivu had to meet the four strict obligations set out by the doctor. The first was reaching his regular playing weight. His protein ratio then had to measure up. During chemotherapy, protein ratios normally drop by up to 15%. Koivu would not play until all his protein ratios returned to higher than normal levels. He then had to test that his energy levels could be quickly replenished following intensive workouts. Finally, Koivu's blood test levels had to come out completely normal, which Koivu finally achieved just hours before stepping on the ice.

Once Koivu had met all the higher bars set for him, Mulder had little choice but to clear him for play.

"What can I say? He met every expectation I purposely set out of reach for him!" Mulder said. "The guy is incredible. His capacity for training hard is superior to anything I've seen up till then. He is an incredibly motivated individual."

Koivu added a pair of assists in the final two regular season games, in which he only took a regular shift. When the playoffs began, he found himself once again on the Canadiens' top line, playing the powerplay unit and killing penalties. The Canadiens would once again stymie the Boston Bruins, second overall in the regular season, before losing to Carolina in six games in the second round. Koivu contributed ten points in twelve playoff games.

The Gainey/Gauthier Regime

Michel Therrien was a fiery coach in junior hockey. His temper got the better of him in the 2002 Conference Semi-Finals against the Carolina Hurricanes. Leading two games to one, and 3-0 in the third period of Game Four, Therrien exploded at referee Kerry Fraser for a call on defenseman Stephane Quintal. After Therrien was warned once already for abusing officials, Fraser did not hesitate in slapping the coach with an extra two-minute minor. The Hurricanes then scored on the ensuing 5 on 3 powerplay, going on to win the game in overtime and the series in six games. The Habs played the rest of the series on their heels. Unable to withstand the Hurricane thrust, they were outscored 17 to 3 in the final seven periods.

The following season, the Canadiens players did not seem to improve. During a 12-game stretch from December to January, the club won but two games and Savard decided to can Therrien. Claude Julien, a coach hired by the Edmonton Oilers organization to lead the Hamilton Bulldogs of the AHL, was brought in to replace him. Julien would win only 12 of 36 games remaining on the season, and the Canadiens would miss the playoffs for the fourth time in five seasons.

With the natives becoming restless in Montreal, Gillette decided it was time to bring about some change. Timmins had restructured the team's scouting department effectively, and Savard had made some minor free agent signings of significance to help the team. Gillette did not wish to lose either man when he brought in former Canadiens captain Bob Gainey to lead the organization. Gainey was named as Executive Vice President and General Manager in June of 2003, and it was immediately felt that he would add some clout and return the tarnished franchise to glory. Savard stepped aside and acted as Gainey's assistant.

Gainey's impact on the team was immediate. His calm demeanor and reassuring manner in dealing with the players, coaches and everyone in the organization helped settle its direction. He was given a five-year contract and preached patience in rebuilding the club brick by brick. He brought and commanded respect for and from his players. After an early preseason game in which defenseman Patrice Brisebois was heartily booed by the locals, Gainey castigated them for their behavior. His influence helped the team to a 16-point improvement in the League standings and an unprecedented first-round upset of the Boston Bruins. Trailing three to one in games, the Canadiens, backed by the strong play of goalie Theodore, beat the odds with three straight wins—a feat never before accomplished in team history. The spent club, however, was undone in four quick games by Tampa in the second round. It was a promising debut under Gainey, and it appeared that this time the Canadiens would not be taking a step backwards the following season.

During the season, several young players, mostly drafted by Houle and Savard, made their first steps with the club. There was Michael Ryder, who should have won the Calder Trophy; Mike Ribeiro, who had lead the team in points at age 23; blossoming defenseman Andrei Markov; and youngsters such as Tomas Plekanec, Chris Higgins and Mike Komisarek, who made their first steps with the team. Equally bright was the return to form of Theodore after an off-season and several off-ice distractions. At the trade deadline, Gainey picked up the enigmatic Alex Kovalev from the Rangers for a song. After a deceiving debut, Kovalev came to life in the playoffs, displaying a skill set Canadiens fans had not seen since the heyday of Guy Lafleur. The future appeared promising, unlike it had in quite some time. Unfortunately, the 2004-05 season was cancelled due to the NHL lockout. A small silver lining would be that many of the team's prospects would receive additional grooming in the minors.

The 2005-06 campaign proved that the Canadiens did not step back. They equaled their point total of 2004, making the playoffs for the first time in successive seasons since 1998. The accomplishment was not without some turbulence along the way. Theodore played poorly and his goals against average swelled by one goal per game. Coach Julien turned to backup Cristobal Huet more often than not, but the move did little to spark the club. Midway through the season, Julien was fired and replaced behind the bench by Gainey, who brought along former Habs player Guy Carbonneau as his assistant. The team was mildly rejuvenated, going 23-15-3 in the second half. Theodore regained the starter's role but continued playing inconsistently. Gainey in turn dispatched the goalie in March to Colorado for David Aebischer, whose best games were the equal of Theodore's worst. The Canadiens met the Hurricanes in the playoffs once more, and again the series took a fateful twist. Having won both games in Carolina, the Canadiens returned home expecting to close out the series. An eye injury to Koivu in Game Three put him out of the playoffs and reduced the Habs' offense to nil. They would score just five goals over the next four games, all one-goal losses.

Expectations were high for 2006-07, but the campaign turned out to be a nightmarish one for the entire Canadiens organization. It began quite well for new Coach Carbonneau, with the team owning a record of 21-8-5 on December 21. Their first-place standing at the time was due to a lethal power play that included such snipers and smooth puck movers as Markov, Kovalev, Ryder and Sheldon Souray, blasting cannonballs from the blue line. Ten players on the team scored in double digits, including youngsters Higgins and Plekanec, who both reached the 20-goal mark.

Tragedy struck the organization on December 8 when it was learned that Bob Gainey's daughter Laura had perished at sea, having been swept overboard while employed on a sailing ship destined for Grenada. Her body was not discovered during a three-day search. Gainey took a leave of absence for a month while assistant Pierre Gauthier ran the club. Sometime over the Christmas season, the Canadiens appeared to lose all momentum. Goalie Huet was injured in February, and the unreliable Aebischer was no solution. The wheels had come off the wagon.

By March 8, the Canadiens' record in their last 35 games was a dismal 12-22-1. Goalie Jaroslav Halak, called up from the Bulldogs, won the starters role and almost salvaged the season. With 13 games remaining and the team rapidly dropping out of the playoff picture, they could ill afford to lose a game. Halak helped the club go on a 9-2 run over the next eleven games. There remained two road games to close out the season, and the Canadiens needed one win to clinch a playoff berth. After Halak lost his next start in New York, Carbonneau curiously handed the most important game of the season to Huet, freshly returned from the injured list. He was given no easy task, having to win in the unfriendly confines of Toronto's Air Canada Centre.

The contest was a roller coaster of emotion. Early in the second period, the Leafs scored to take a 3-1 lead. Then Michael Ryder powered the Canadiens, with a natural hat trick in the span of 5:49. Toronto then pulled starter Andrew Raycroft for little-used substitute Jean-Sebastien Aubin, who surrendered a fifth goal minutes later. Montreal appeared in command before Toronto added a goal late in the second frame. The Canadiens' lack of discipline the rest of the way cost them the game and their season. Just as the second period ended, Steve Begin was assessed a four-minute high-sticking penalty, and the Leafs capitalized 28 seconds into the third period. Koivu then went to the box for tripping, and Toronto added another to take the lead. For the remainder of the game, they clamped down on the Canadiens, keeping them to three shots. The Canadiens headed home for the summer a very disillusioned group.

Trevor Timmins had done an enviable job recruiting and developing talent for the team, and the Canadiens owned several prospects and young players whose futures boded well for the franchise. Added to youngsters Ryder, Halak, Higgins, Plekanec and Komisarek was a group of up and comers that included Andrei and Sergei Kostitsyn, Guillaume Latendresse, Ryan O'Byrne, Maxim Lapierre, and Mark Streit. It was as strong a crop of talent as any since 1986. Standing head and shoulders above in promise was 20-year-old goaltender Carey Price, who had just completed a season in which he was both a gold medalist and MVP in the World Junior Tournament and a Calder Cup winner and MVP with the AHL Bulldogs. Chosen 5th overall in the 2005 draft, the Canadiens' future rested on his potential. To no one's surprise, Price made the club at training camp in 2007.

With plenty of time on their hands for off-season soul-searching, the Canadiens regrouped and achieved unexpected heights in 2007-08. Their first-place finish in the Eastern Conference was their strongest regular season showing since 1989. Despite the loss of Souray to free agency, the Canadiens' power play didn't skip a beat, with defenseman Streit making a seamless transition to the unit. Markov and Kovalev put in their strongest seasons with the team, and Tomas Plekanec had developed into a solid two-way pivot. The Habs again met the Bruins in the first round, and the eighth-place Boston squad gave Montreal all it could handle in a seven-game set. The Canadiens emerged victorious but drained. Fans' dreams of a 25th Stanley Cup, however, quickly went by the wayside with a five-game loss to the Flyers in the second round.

There was little discouragement following the season. It was felt that the Canadiens were poised to join the NHL elite and that they were more popular than ever with fans. The Bell Centre finally felt like home and hosted its 100th consecutive sellout during the season. George Gillette was an abundantly happy owner. The Canadiens' estimated franchise worth had grown in successive seasons, and the team was about to enter its centennial season as potential Stanley Cup aspirants.

To celebrate the team's hundredth year, a season-long party had long been in the planning. Every manner of festivity was undertaken, from jersey retirement ceremonies to hosting the NHL Draft and All-Star Game. Memorabilia to suit every demand was sold: there were commemorative DVDs and books, replica jerseys, a monopoly board game and even a movie. Banners emblazoned with the centennial logo hung throughout the city's downtown core, featuring pairs of players past and present, symbolic to the passing of the torch. There was Lafleur and Kovalev, Dryden and Price, and

Béliveau and Koivu. Very little about the celebrations was subtle. It placed enormous pressure on the players to perform. The expectations of a Stanley Cup were unreal and beyond idealistic.

To help bolster the team's chances, Gainey traded for forwards Robert Lang and Alex Tanguay, and both made smooth transitions into the lineup. Everything was proceeding according to plan, with the Canadiens near the top of their division days before the All-Star break. An impressive record of 27-11-6 had created a frenzied feeling among fans dreaming the Cup drought was at its end.

The dream did not last long, though. Players, who had been pushed hard and had become overly taxed, broke down. Injuries sent the team off the rails, and the pressure translated into dressing room schisms. The Canadiens went through a 15-game stretch, winning only three. After a 6-2 loss in Calgary, Carbonneau took the team bowling to ease tensions and bring about a modicum of camaraderie. They responded with a 7-2 loss the next night. Carbonneau finally seemed to have settled things with a four-game win streak in late February, but Gainey decided to fire his coach and took over behind the bench a second time. He guided the club to 6-6-4 finish, but the team hit the playoffs appearing disinterested and uninspired. Crowning its centennial was a four-game sweep at the hands of the rival Bruins.

In the off-season, Gainey cleaned house, allowing 11 free agents to walk, including Koivu, Kovalev, Komisarek, Tanguay and Lang. He would use the freed-up cap space to go on a signing spree, completely reconstituting the team's composition. The undertaking would be dubbed a chemistry experiment. When free agency opened on July 1, Gainey and the Canadiens were big spenders. They brought in 40-goal scorer Mike Cammalleri from Calgary, diminutive sniper Brian Gionta from New Jersey, grinding forward Travis Moen from San Jose, and defensemen Hal Gill and Jaroslav Spacek from Pittsburgh and Buffalo, respectively. On the day prior, Gainey traded Higgins and valuable prospect Ryan McDonagh to the Rangers for center Scott Gomez. To guide all this smallish offensive weaponry, he had signed Coach Jacques Martin, a known defensive strategist.

Gainey's chemistry experiment was largely deemed as a failure through 82 games. The team was dysfunctional for the most part, unable to seemingly commit itself to Martin's system for any length of time. The newer players were still finding their places among veteran team members, and with no captain named for the season to replace Koivu, all voices had a say. One disenchanted member uttered one comment too many for Gainey's liking and was sent home with pay and bought out at season's end. Goalie Price had a difficult season. The young netminder had seen his play slip since the previous year's All-Star game. The team turned to backup Jaroslav Halak, who had openly declared through his agent that he wanted the starter's job. Subsequently, Gainey called it quits and passed the mantle to Pierre Gauthier. Gainey would remain with the club in executive and consultant roles.

The Canadiens' 39-33-10 record was barely good enough for eighth place, and clinching a playoff spot proved quite dramatic when they failed in winning any of their last three games. Entering the playoffs through the proverbial back door, the team prepared for what all the hockey cognoscente figured to be a bulldozing sweep at the hands of the offensively gifted Washington Capitals. Prior to the start of the series, a feud that had been ongoing throughout the season erupted into a full-blown splitting of factions on the team. Forward Gomez, proposing that the Canadiens play a more freewheeling style, butted heads with defenseman Gill, who thought they ought to play as instructed by Martin. A tug of war between disciples on both sides continued as the series began. The Canadiens surprised everyone by taking the first game 3-2 in overtime, playing as close to Martin's teachings as possible. They were ahead in the second game but lost it in overtime when they strayed from their system. The fissure continued over the next two games, both losses in which they were outscored by an 11-4 margin. With their backs to the wall, the players realized that they could hardly beat the Capitals at their own game. Prior to the fifth game, it had been decided that they would return to a more defensive form.

The story beginning with Game Five became the outstanding play of goalie Halak. With the team increasingly conscious of play in its own zone, they fortified their puck stopper, blocking shots and eliminating passing lanes. Washington players were frustrated and becoming undisciplined. The Canadiens protected a one-goal lead

Carey Price, goaltender for the Montreal Canadiens. *Author: Vava manouche*

for 36 minutes, and Halak stopped 37 of 38 shots for a 2-1 win. Most importantly, the Habs had found their game. With all players finally on the same page, they would rarely waver from it in coming weeks. Back at the Bell Centre two nights later, Halak and the Canadiens put in a performance for the ages. Cammalleri scored his fourth and fifth goals of the postseason, and Halak made a resounding 53 saves in a 4-1 victory. With the series now tied, the pressure shifted completely onto the psychologically frail Capitals.

A scenario similar to Game Five played out in the deciding match in Washington. The Canadiens built up a two-goal lead and hung on as the Caps threw all they could at Halak. He finally conceded a goal with less than three minutes remaining in the game, but the Canadiens held out for a 2-1 win. Following the game, a desolate crew of Capitals snipers had no idea what had hit them. It seemed to them like the Canadiens had jumped on every error they made while the buttressed Halak stood tall.

The defending Cup champion Pittsburgh Penguins were up next, and over the course of seven games, the Canadiens proceeded to pick them apart just as they had done with their previous opponent. The teams traded wins for the first six games, with Montreal evening the series three times. Halak continued his brilliance, and Cammalleri kept up his timely scoring. Just as importantly, center Plekanec threw a blanket over the League's best player, reducing Sydney Crosby to a goal and three helpers in the series. The Canadiens then met their match against the Philadelphia Flyers. Big, strong and impenetrable, the Flyers clogged up the middle of the ice, and the Canadiens were ill-equipped to pierce their armor. It was the farthest the Canadiens had gone in the playoffs since last winning the Cup in 1993, but the party would be over in five short games. The Flyers were on a mission, and they shut out the Canadiens in three games. The dream season was at an end.

With minimal retooling by Gauthier, the Canadiens prepared to aim high for 2010-11. In the off-season, Gauthier settled the goaltending controversy by choosing to send Halak to St. Louis for a center of size named Lars Eller. Early in the campaign, defenseman Markov went down to injury and Gauthier sacrificed no roster players in replacing him with James Wisniewski. Montreal finished sixth in the East, improving by eight points over the previous season. Carey Price appeared to return to his former self, while rookie defenseman P.K. Subban made an impression that left few opponents indifferent.

Like an old movie script, springtime for the Canadiens began with a game against the Bruins. This time, however, it would be Boston directing the movie. After the Canadiens took the first two games on the road, the Bruins returned the favor, winning both games in Montreal. Back in Boston, the Bruins took the fifth game in double overtime, winning 2-1. But the feisty Canadiens were not about to bow down, winning by the same tally back at the Bell Centre. A thriller was set for the seventh game, and the climax played out as dramatically as any series between the clubs. The Bruins were leading 3-2 late in the game, when Subban tied it with a power play goal with less than two minutes on the clock. The game headed to overtime once more and was settled when a Nathan Horton shot from the blue line deflected past Price.

There was great promise heading into 2011-12, and there was no reason to see it otherwise. The Canadiens had come within a goal of eliminating the eventual Cup champs. There was much to build upon. The Canadiens had talented youth at all positions joined by a core of skillful veterans. Added to the latter in the off-season was triggerman Eric Cole.

Gauthier made several moves beginning with the dismissal of assistant coach Perry Pearn early in the season. Due to Markov's unscheduled late return from injury, the power play was a mess and Pearn took the bullet. Steady rearguard Jaroslav Spacek was then dealt to Carolina for Tomas Kaberle. When the team hadn't settled itself 32 games into the season, Gauthier dismissed Coach Martin, whose record of 13-12-7 still placed the team on the perimeter of the playoff picture with 50 games to go. He then replaced Martin with assistant Randy Cunneyworth, who, according to the Montreal media, also committed the unforgivable sin of being English, and ran a system that was practically identical to that of his mentor. Two days following his hire, Gauthier clarified his move, tagging him as an interim coach.

When Mike Cammalleri bared his soul and spoke out negatively regarding the team approaching games as though they played not to lose, Gauthier decided to trade him mid-game. Many of the Canadiens' problems on the season were easily attributed to a lack of healthy contributors. There were numerous injuries all season, and though the Canadiens kept their heads up through many losses, regular line combinations were practically impossible to achieve. Sixteen losses came in overtime or by shootout, and many others were by the slimmest of margins. Despite the team finishing 15th in the East, Carey Price played about as well as could be expected, rarely surrendering five goals in a game all season.

The team's fans were disenchanted. With just two games left in the season, Gauthier was dismissed.

Hope Springs Eternal

When Canadiens' owner Geoff Molson undertook a search for a new GM, he needed to find a good hockey man, a person who blended well with those working beneath him. He wanted a strong, likable communicator, who understood that no one man will ever own all the answers. He found these qualities in Blackhawks assistant GM Marc Bergevin.

Bergevin started off fresh, with the same clean slate all new managers have. New regimes, in hockey and in any sport, begin with large measures of hope. Often that hope isn't very palpable, but given Bergevin's traits, initial moves and what he has to work with in terms of team elements, there are very encouraging reasons for optimism.

The Canadiens of 2011-12, who finished 15th in the Eastern Conference, own little in common with virtually every last-place team in hockey history.

First of all, they ended up placed where they finished due to a ridiculous number of man games lost to injuries. That is no excuse, just a plain fact. Despite collateral losses of talent, the Canadiens finished second in the league in penalty killing, with a ratio of 88.6. Last-place teams are rarely top ten in any category, let alone second.

Again, this is not your usual last-place club. Generally, NHL bottom feeders have a dearth of talent, low payrolls, few promising prospects, little in terms of offensive frontline talent and an arena filled with empty seats. Purchase a game ticket, and you'll receive a coupon for a free beer and hot dog.

This does not describe the Canadiens by any stretch. They have a wealth of talent, they spend to the cap limit annually, are well stocked with prospects, own a top line which 25 NHL teams would love to brag about and they sell out their arena on a consistent basis. The price of a beer and hot dog at the Bell Centre is half the price of game tickets for most bottom-feeding clubs.

The talent is all that matters in assessing club potential moving forward. There is a veteran core in place, with Gionta and Cole on the wings. Cole is coming off a season in which he achieved career highs on a last-place team. Gionta was absent for much of 2012 but can be penciled in for 25 goals when healthy. On defense, Josh Gorges is a warrior on the penalty kill and one of the League's top shot blockers. Andrei Markov is a power play quarterback with few peers. Carey Price is a young veteran in goal who has yet to peak. At age 25, he has more NHL game experience than any goalie since Martin Brodeur. At center, the Canadiens have Tomas Plekanec, who may sacrifice offense come playoff time, but has proven capable of shutting down players such as Crosby, Ovechkin and others in the postseason.

The younger core is comprised of such talents as Subban, Eller, David Desharnais and Max Pacioretty. Subban, in only two seasons, has already proven to be a consumer of large game minutes. He plays all three units, and brings a dimension on defense that Canadiens have not had since the departure of Chris Chelios. Desharnais and Pacioretty, in their first full seasons, contributed 60 points and 33 goals respectively. Eller, as a third line center, counted 16 goals while playing in a mostly defensive role.

And there is a plentitude of promising assets moving forward. Jarred Tinordi, Morgan Ellis and Nathan Beaulieu were all number-one defensemen on teams that played in the 2012 Memorial Cup. Center Michaël Bournival captained the team that won the tournament. Winger Brendan Gallagher was a leading scorer on the Canadian team that won a silver medal at the 2012 World Junior Championship. Louis Leblanc, a gritty and intelligent forward, already has a half season of NHL experience and will only get better. Alex Galchenyuk, drafted by the Canadiens as the third overall pick in the 2012 draft, could become one of the rare players in team history to make the club as an 18-year-old.

Beyond the bevy of talent, there is plentiful hope in Bergevin himself. A journeyman player in his time, he seems to have been blessed with an absence of oversized ego. He impressed upon his hire, stating in a press conference that he does not expect to have every answer to every solution. He would surround himself with those who may have, then consult, listen and decide. His role, as he saw it, was as a member of a management team.

Amidst a firing line of questions from the Montreal press, Bergevin made a pair of intelligently potent declarations. When asked about potential coaches for the team, he replied that coaches, unlike players, get better with age and experience. Players have a physical timeline that determines when they peak, but coaches do not have similar mental restrictions. In regards to young prospects, Bergevin alluded to players who had been rushed to the NHL and the fact that the timing hampered their fuller development. His astute answer spoke volumes regarding his patience and composure. Prospects are only ever criticized when hurried to the big leagues; no one ever complains by suggesting they were left to groom too long in the minor leagues.

In the off-season free agency frenzy, he tackled one aspect of the club that needed an upgrade. He addressed the club's lack of physicality and aggressiveness with the signings of Brandon Prust, Colby Armstrong and Francis Bouillon.

Over the summer, Bergevin filled out his hockey department with a half dozen new hires, several of them in positions that had not existed previously. He'll have not one, but two assistant general managers. An additional third assistant coach will work from the press box. Player-specific positions were created to lighten Timmins's load, and three individuals are now tasked with the coaching, development and directing aspects of the organization. Despite the numerous new areas, no one will trip over one another in their defined roles in Montreal and Hamilton. When Bergevin emphasized that he would work as part of a team, few realized at the time how many positions required filling. He would not spread himself thin as his predecessors had.

His entire hockey operations department is not unlike those employed by Sam Pollock so long ago, wherein many lieutenants worked behind the scenes. As Geoff Molson no doubt recalled, there was a man for every task. Claude Ruel, Ron Caron, Al MacNeil, Cliff Fletcher and others, each had specific roles to play in numerous Canadiens conquests. Coming from a Cup-winning organization that included Scotty Bowman, Bergevin learned that such thinking was perhaps costly, but worth it, necessary, and not at all obsolete.

Bergevin may also have taken other management cues from Pollock. Weeks prior to filling out his organization, Bergevin happened upon a coaching choice he felt was perfectly suited to all angles of the task that lie ahead.

In polls conducted by the Montreal press, and on radio talk shows, that coach Michel Therrien was nowhere near a popular choice. The fans spoke loudly that moving forward cannot be achieved by turning back in time for a re-treaded coach. The voice of public opinion had spoken.

In the great tradition of Sam Pollock, Bergevin ignored the naysayers and followed his better informed inclinations and hired Therrien regardless.

The future, indeed, looks bright.

BIBLIOGRAPHY

Barette, Rosaire. *Leo Dandurand, Sportsman.* Le Droit; Ottawa, 1952.

Beddoes, Dick. *Greatest Hockey Stories.* MacMillan of Canada; Toronto, 1990.

Brunet, Mathias. *Mario Tremblay: Le Bagarreur.* Québec Amérique; Montreal, 1997.

Bruneau, Pierre, and Normand, Léandre. *La Glorieuse Histoire des Canadiens.* Éditions de l'Homme; Montreal, 2003.

Carrier, Roch. *Our Life With The Rocket: The Maurice Richard Story.* Penguin Books Canada; Toronto, 2001.

Coleman, Charles. *1893-1926 Volume 1 of Trail of the Stanley Cup.* National Hockey League; 1966.

Cox, Damian and Stellick, Gord. *'67: The Maple Leafs, Their Sensational Victory, and the End of an Empire.* John Wiley & Sons; 2006.

Cruise, David, and Griffiths, Allison. *Net Worth.* Viking Canada; 1991.

Denault, Todd. *Jacques Plante: The Man Who Changed the Face of Hockey.* McLellan and Stewart; Toronto, 2009.

Dryden, Ken. *The Game: A Reflective and thought provoking look at life in hockey,* MacMillan of Canada; Toronto, 1983.

Duplacey, James and Wilkens, Charles. *Forever Rivals: Montreal Canadiens and Toronto Maple Leafs.* Random House; Toronto, 1996.

Fisher, Red. *Hockey, Heroes, and Me.* MacMillan of Canada; Toronto, 1994.

Fischler, Stan and Shirley. *Heroes and History: Voices from the NHL's Past.* McGraw-Hill Ryerson; Whitby, Ontario, 1994.

Frayne, Trent. *The Mad Men of Hockey*. McLellan and Stewart; Toronto, 1974.

Geoffrion, Bernard, and Fischler, Stan. *Boom Boom: The Life and Times of Bernard Geoffrion*. McGraw-Hill Ryerson; Whitby, Ontario, 1997.

Germain, Georges-Hébert. *Overtime: The Legend of Guy Lafleur*. Penguin Books Canada; Toronto, 1990

Goyens, Chrys, and Turowetz, Allan. *Lions In Winter*. Prentice-Hall Canada; Toronto, 1986.

Hunter, Douglas. *Scotty Bowman: A Life in Hockey*. Penguin Books Canada; Toronto, 1998.

Irvin, Dick. *The Habs: An Oral History of the Montreal Canadiens, 1940-1980*. MacMillan of Canada; Toronto, 1991.

Irvin, Dick. *Behind the Bench*. MacMillan of Canada; Toronto, 1993

Jenish, D'Arcy. *Montreal Canadiens: 100 Years of Glory*. Doubleday Canada, Toronto, 2008.

Kitchen, Paul. *Win, Tie or Wrangle: The Inside Story of the Old Ottawa Senators*. Penumbra Press; Manotick, Ontario, 2009.

Leonetti, Mike. *Hockey's Golden Era Stars of the Original Six*. MacMillan of Canada; Toronto, 1993.

McFarlane, Brian. *The Habs: True Hockey Stories*. Prosporo Books Canada; Toronto, 2008.

Mouton, Claude. *The Montreal Canadiens*. Key Porter Books; Toronto, 1987.

National Hockey League: *Official Guide and Record Book* 2000 - 2010

Quarrington, Paul. *Original Six*. Reed Books Canada; Toronto, 1996.

Richard, Maurice, and Fischler, Stan. *Flying Frenchmen: Hockey's Greatest Dynasty*. Prentice-Hall Canada; Toronto, 1974.

Robinson, Dean. *Howie Morenz: Hockey's First Superstar*. Boston Mills Press; Erin Mills Ontario, 1982.

Robinson, Larry, with Goyens, Chrys. *Robinson for the Defense*. McGraw-Hill Ryerson; Toronto, 1982.

Roy, Michel. *Patrick Roy: Winning, Nothing Else*. Wiley & Sons; 2008.

Selke, Frank J., with H. Gordon Green. *Behind the Cheering*. MacMillan of Canada; Toronto, 1962.

Young, Scott and Astrid. *O'Brien: From Water Boy to One Million a Year*. Ryerson Press; Toronto, 1967.

Young, Scott. Conn Smythe: *If You Can't Beat 'Em In The Alley....* McLellan and Stewart; Toronto, 1981.

Newspapers, Magazines and Websites
La Patrie
La Presse
Le Canada
Le Journal de Montreal
Le Devoir
Saturday Night
Sports Illustrated
The Montreal Herald
The Montreal Gazette
The Ottawa Citizen
The Pittsburgh Press
The Toronto Star
www.hockeyreference.com
www.sihrhockey.org